We all put off making plans sometimes, and it seems the mor⋯
more likely we have put off creating a plan. This clear and useful book helps families see
that it is never too late to plan a better future for an adult with disabilities. Most of all,
as a parent, I like the book because it is realistic. I believe many families will find the help
they need here.

> —Sue Swenson, executive director of the Arc of the United States
> and former commissioner for developmental disabilities during the
> Clinton administration

With a host of practical ideas, examples, and creative, do-able steps, Judith Greenbaum has
used her experience as a parent and a professional to fashion a resource that is particularly
useful for planning for the future. It will help families who too often have been the sole
caregivers, but who now need others to know their sons and daughters as they do. Families
need others to work in partnership with them in planning and shaping living, working,
and caregiving relationships that form the foundation for meaningful lives. Greenbaum
respects and honors the needs of everyone involved: parents, siblings, adult children with
disabilities, and direct caregivers. She outlines an empowering path to address both the
dreams and fears of a future none of us controls.

> —Bill Gaventa, M.Div., is associate professor of pediatrics at the
> Robert Wood Johnson Medical School/UMDNJ and director of
> community and congregational supports at the Elizabeth M. Boggs
> Center on Developmental Disabilities

For someone with developmental disabilities and for his or her parents, the world changes abruptly once that person graduates from school. Gone are guiding laws and procedures and guaranteed choices. The person with developmental disabilities and the family are essentially on their own, facing a jigsaw puzzle of possible services, with very few guarantees. Greenbaum's book is an enormous help in this venture, and I enthusiastically recommend it, not just for parents, but also for service providers trying to help in these crucial transitions. While Greenbaum is knowledgeable about the latest thinking in the disability field, she is neither biased nor dogmatic; her suggestions accommodate a great variety of family preferences and experiences.

—Martha Ziegler, national autism consultant with Youth Advocate Programs, Inc., and parent of an adult daughter with autism

This is essential reading for parents and siblings of adults with developmental disabilities who are considering their options for long-term planning. Greenbaum offers specific information on the options available to adults with developmental disabilities while also pointing readers to strategies for creating flexible arrangements that best suit the needs of their family member. As the sibling of an adult with developmental disabilities, this book helped me understand the importance of developing a life plan alongside my brother and parents to best ensure a happy, full, productive and sustainable future for us all.

—Emily Bloom, MA, sister of a brother with developmental disabilities who lives an independent life

I wish we had had a guide like this years ago when we were struggling to find resources to help my developmentally disabled son access good services. This book brings realistic and practical suggestions to solve our present problems. It offers ways to plan for the future of our son and other developmentally disabled adults to insure a quality life when we are no longer able to advocate for them.

—Janet A. Birk, registered nurse and parent of a son with severe developmental disabilities

Life Planning

for Adults with Developmental Disabilities

A Guide for Parents
& Family Members

JUDITH GREENBAUM, PH.D.

New Harbinger Publications, Inc.

Publisher's Note

Distributed in Canada by Raincoast Books

Copyright © 2007 by Judith Greenbaum
New Harbinger Publications, Inc.
5674 Shattuck Avenue
Oakland, CA 94609
www.newharbinger.com

Acquired by Melissa Kirk; Cover design by Amy Shoup;
Edited by Jasmine Star; Text design by Tracy Carlson

Library of Congress Cataloging-in-Publication Data

Greenbaum, Judith.
  Life planning for adults with developmental disabilities : a guide for parents and family members / Judith Greenbaum.
    p. cm.
  Includes bibliographical references and index.
  ISBN-13: 978-1-57224-451-1 (alk. paper)
  ISBN-10: 1-57224-451-8 (alk. paper)
  1. Developmentally disabled--Services for--United States. 2. Developmentally disabled--Family relation-
ships. 3. Parents of children with disabilities--United States. 4. Parent and adult child. I. Title.
  HV1570.5.U65G74 2007
  362.3'8--dc22
                              2007005762

09 08 07

10 9 8 7 6 5 4 3 2 1

First printing

To my children
Dan Greenbaum and Alice Beresen
Josh Greenbaum and Keren Stronach
Sara Greenbaum and Darryl Sherman
Susannah (Susie) Greenbaum

and

To Leonard

Contents

Acknowledgments

I would like to thank the many people who shared their thoughts and feelings with me.

The families whose inspiration, courage, and generosity made this book possible: Janet Birk, Dan Roberts and Lisa Roberts, Joni Thiele and Mitchel Thiele, Lois and Jim Montague and Jerod Montague, Jill Barker, Pat and Barb O'Donnell, Ann and David Saffer and Sarah Saffer, Bob Meyer, Chuck and Basti Jenkins, Jane Peterson, Kelly Crawford, Caren Jobe and Sam Jobe, Mildred Ostrowski and Marnie Diamond, Jeff Hopkins, William Nee, Mary O'Riordan, and Susie Greenbaum.

The direct care workers and supervisors whose ongoing commitment, dedication, and just plain hard work enhance the lives of adults with developmental disabilities: Penny Dombrowski, Bill Potter, Kathy Robles, Andrea McCrum, Irma Ojeda, Barb Vernier, Shori Teeple, and Barbara Scheel-Ayers.

The Washtenaw County Community Support and Treatment Services staff, who juggle mandates and money in order to provide services to adults with developmental disabilities: Donna Sabourin, director; Trish Cortes; Edie Gentner; and Lydia Sattler.

Sherry Fernandez, executive director of the Washtenaw Association for Community Advocacy, the Arc of Michigan.

And the Daughters of St. Mary of Providence and the Servants of Charity for the loving care they provide my daughter Susie.

Introduction

I have written this book for parents like myself, who are getting on in years and who are beginning to worry once again about what will happen to their adult son or daughter with developmental disabilities after they are gone. This book is also for siblings and other family members who are concerned with the well-being of these adults. Some of us are already in various stages of planning for the future. Others don't know where to begin. We all want the best for our sons and daughters, but we may not know what that is or how to make it happen. We fear the worst, and it often paralyzes us.

The information in this book can be the first weapon against fear. Armed with information about various living situations and work and recreational options, parents and other family members can begin contemplating the future with optimism and hope.

Defining Developmental Disability

Generally, "developmental disability" refers to epilepsy, autism, mental retardation, or cerebral palsy that is relatively severe. Under certain circumstances, the term can also refer to traumatic brain injury, severe behavioral problems, and severe learning disabilities. Developmental disabilities can run the gamut from relatively mild to severe, depending on the person's functional limitations and need for support.

In the Developmental Disabilities Assistance and Bill of Rights Act of 2000, the federal government defines developmental disabilities as follows:

> The term "developmental disability" means a severe, chronic disability of an individual that
>
> ■ is attributable to a mental or physical impairment or combination of mental and physical impairments

- is manifested before the person attains age twenty-two

- is likely to continue indefinitely

- results in substantial functional limitations in three or more of the following areas of major life activity:

  - self-care

  - receptive and expressive language

  - learning

  - mobility

  - self-direction

  - capacity for independent living

  - economic self-sufficiency

- reflects the person's need for ... special interdisciplinary ... services, individualized supports, or other forms of assistance that are of lifelong or of extended duration and are individually planned and coordinated

Who This Book Is For

This book is not only for parents and families of adults with developmental disabilities as defined in the law (meaning epilepsy, autism, mental retardation, and cerebral palsy). It can also be used by families of people with other disabilities, such as severe mental illness, muscular dystrophy, and other relatively severe genetic and acquired disabilities. Although our children may be quite different from one another, we all have similar worries about the future.

Why I Wrote This Book

This book is the outgrowth of both my professional career and my personal experience as the mother of a forty-three-year-old daughter with developmental disabilities. I have been a professional in the field of special education for over thirty years, working as a consultant to school districts and as a trainer of teachers and other school professionals. I have worked with many parents during that time, providing them with information and strategies to help their children both at home and in school. I've also served as a family advocate and am well versed in the special education laws that serve children with various disabilities and impairments from ages three to twenty-one, or from birth to age twenty-six in some states.

My daughter Susie is the youngest of my four children. She functions in the moderate to severe range of mental retardation. Until about five years ago, I had only given vague thought to her future. She had been living at Our Lady of Providence Center (OLP) in Northville, Michigan, for the previous twenty years. Susie came home on alternate weekends and for long holidays, and because OLP was just a half hour away, I could see her anytime I wanted to. I thought this situation would go on forever, but on a muggy evening in August 2000, Sister Linda gave parents the shocking news that OLP was closing the following April. We had nine months to make other arrangements for our daughters. This book is the outgrowth of those nine frustrating months during which the other parents and I tried to negotiate the often uncoordinated and confusing world of community services for adults with developmental disabilities.

Susie is now living in a good but interim situation, and she'll eventually move to another state to be near one of her brothers or her sister. We're still in the process of deciding where and how. So, in a way, you and I are on a journey together, although we may be in different stages of planning.

Susie's father, Leonard, died when Susie was nine years old. He was an amazingly loving and supportive father to all his children, and his death left a terrible void in my life. I raised my children alone for ten years. Then, at a fundraiser for Our Lady of Providence Center, I met Dan, whose daughter Lisa you'll meet in this book. We've been together for many years, and Lisa has become a daughter to me. Many parents of children with developmental disabilities have to go it alone, which can make an already difficult situation even more challenging, to say the least. If this is your situation, perhaps you'll find another partner, as I did after many years. But either way, the most important thing is to find some strength within yourself to continue—and to prevail.

Throughout the book, I'll share my own experiences as well as those of other parents as we all work our way through the planning process. I'll present some of the recent research on adults with developmental disabilities and their families to help you make the most informed decisions. You'll also meet many adults with different developmental disabilities, including my daughter Susie, as they go about their lives. Each is a unique individual, with an individual pattern of strengths and weaknesses. They live and work in different situations with different amounts of support from community agencies. Their lives will serve to illustrate the various alternatives you have and the obstacles you face when trying to decide on the best living and working situation for your son or daughter.

How to Use This Book

Although this book is also for siblings and other family members who want to do the best they can to help their loved one live a rich and satisfying life, for simplicity's sake I'll assume you are a parent and refer to "your son or daughter." But this in no way excludes anyone, particularly a sibling, who is trying to assist in life planning for an adult with developmental disabilities. Also for simplicity's sake, I'll refer to the adult with disabilities as your adult child or your child, terms we use for all our adult children. But it is important to remember that we are talking about adults, not children.

Because each state uses different names for the various governmental agencies that provide services, supports, and funding to adults with disabilities, I've used the generic term "community agency" throughout the book when referring to these agencies. In addition to federal and state agencies mandated by law, there are private, nonprofit agencies that governmental agencies contract with to provide the staff your son or daughter needs to function well at home, at work, and in other community activities. Finally, there are both parent organizations and consumer organizations, made up of parents and families of children and adults with disabilities, as well as the adults with disabilities themselves, who can provide information and advocacy for parents and families. (Chapter 9 will provide more information about the various agencies and organizations and what each does.)

The first four chapters of this book will help you fine-tune the current situation, both yours and your son's or daughter's, making no major changes. The rest of the book focuses on helping you make plans for the future.

Chapter 1 gives a brief overview of the recent history of the parents' movement and changes in the situation of people with disabilities brought about by society's changing views of people with disabilities. It also sums up the changes in family dynamics as the child with disabilities progresses from adolescence through adulthood.

Chapter 2 focuses on taking an inventory of how things are going in your life at this time, assessing the situation of both the adult with developmental disabilities and the parents. Many parents are putting in long, hard hours helping their son or daughter, often to their own detriment.

Chapter 3 helps parents enhance their own quality of life. By helping yourself, you'll be in a better position to help your son or daughter. You'll also be able to gather the strength and clarity to make good plans for your child's future. Chapter 4 describes different ways you and your family can encourage your son or daughter to take on an adult role. It will also help you improve your son's or daughter's quality of life in the interim, as you develop a long-term plan.

Chapter 5 begins the planning process by helping you and your family describe your son's or daughter's interests, preferences, and needs, with the input of your son or daughter. This person-centered plan forms the basis for all other plans for the future.

Chapter 6 provides information about various residential options you and your son or daughter can consider in order to decide on the best living situation. Chapter 7 discusses the importance of work and other meaningful activities in the life of the adult with developmental disabilities, presenting various work options as well as recreational activities that can help fill the day. Chapter 8 provides information that will help you select a professional caregiver who will be a good person to take care of your child. Chapter 9 describes the functions of various community agencies that provide support and services to people with disabilities and their families and also answers some questions about these agencies. It provides practical advice on how to interact with these agencies in order to develop an appropriate service plan for your son or daughter.

Chapter 10 will help you put it all together into a plan for your child's future. It will also help you document that plan so that others will be aware of your wishes and all of the details involved. And finally, you can use the Resources section at the end of the book, which includes a list of helpful Web sites, to gather more information.

Some Helpful Definitions

Before you move ahead into the rest of the book, let me define a few terms I'll be using. Some of you will undoubtedly already be familiar with many if not all of the terms below. Although all of these terms will be defined later in the book in the appropriate context, here are a few definitions to help you through the early chapters:

Community agency: A community agency is a publicly funded agency which, by law, provides services and the funding for services to a variety of people in need, including adults with disabilities.

Provider agencies: A provider agency is a private, nonprofit employment agency set up specifically to provide direct care workers, job coaches, and personal assistants to people with disabilities, under contract with a community agency.

Direct care worker: Direct care workers are trained by community agencies and provider agencies to provide care to people with disabilities.

Parent organizations: Parent organizations, such as the Arc and United Cerebral Palsy, are made up of parents and families of children and adults with disabilities. They provide information and advocacy for these families.

SSDI (Social Security Disability Insurance): SSDI provides funding to people with relatively severe disabilities who are the sons or daughters of retired or deceased workers or who themselves were workers who became disabled. People with disabilities who are eligible for SSDI are also eligible for both Medicare and Medicaid, regardless of age.

SSI (Supplemental Security Income):   SSI provides funding to low-income people with disabilities who can't work full time to support themselves due to the severity of their disabilities. Most people with severe disabilities fit into the low-income category since, in general, their parents' income is not counted for eligibility purposes.

Medicaid: Medicaid provides health care for low-income people. It also provides funding for direct care workers, health aides, and personal assistants for people with disabilities.

Hopefully this book will help you move along in the planning process. Developing a workable plan for the future will allay many of your fears about what will become of your son or daughter. And making a plan for your son's or daughter's future may be the most important gift you can give your child.

CHAPTER 1

A Look at the Past and the Present

As the parent of an adult with developmental disabilities, you've been given a monumentally difficult task, but you've seen it through, often with little help, for a long, long time. You have been a caregiver with less fanfare and more grace than most people give you credit for. Through the years you have acted as teacher, nurse, and advocate for your child with developmental disabilities, often having to fight for appropriate educational, medical, and support services.

Brothers and sisters of individuals with disabilities have also performed yeoman duty when it comes to supporting their sibling. They have helped care for, teach, and protect their sibling, often acting as assistant parents. They've had to share their parents with a needy brother or sister who often took up more than his or her fair share of parental time and love, and who may well continue to do so. Though it wasn't easy for them, they generally rose to the occasion and became better people for it (Powell and Ogle 1985). Today they stand side by side with their parents, often encouraging their parents to take the first steps in planning for the future.

Having an adult child with developmental disabilities has presented many challenges through the years. You may have worried about whether you were doing your best for your child with disabilities. Now you worry about the future. As a parent of a forty-three-year-old daughter with developmental disabilities, I share these feelings.

You may have managed fairly well so far, but as is inevitable, you're getting older. As time passes, it may become more difficult for you to provide the level of care you have in the past, and it's likely that the day will come when you're not around to make or participate in decisions about your child's life. It is time to take stock and begin making plans for the future.

A Brief History of Legal Issues and Social Attitudes

We've made enormous strides in establishing and protecting the legal rights of people with developmental disabilities during my lifetime. Society has become more accepting of children and adults with disabilities, and they have become part of our daily lives. Like me, you may have been born into an earlier, less tolerant era, and you may need some reassurance that things have changed. So before we start the process of taking inventory of your child's current situation (and yours) and developing a plan for your child's future, let's take a look at the transformation that's occurred over recent decades.

Institutionalization

Before 1960, parents of children with developmental disabilities were told to institutionalize the child at birth, "for the good of both child and family." And at the urging of doctors and family, most parents did so. But some brave parents didn't accept this harsh philosophy and kept their children at home, at least for a while, despite the fact that no one knew what to do with these children.

An example from my own life often reminds me of the world as it was then for children with developmental disabilities and their parents: In the 1940s, when I was about twelve years old, I remember passing a dark window with the curtains drawn as I walked to school with my friends. Occasionally I noticed that the curtain was pulled aside, and then, as I looked, it would drop back into place. I mentioned this several times to David, a friend who lived in the large apartment house with the mysterious window, but he usually dismissed me with a soft shrug. One day he finally told me, sadly, that it was his little brother, who had Down syndrome. He added that his brother never went out of the house because his parents were afraid that someone would take him away and institutionalize him if they knew of his existence, and in fact, many do-gooders did just that sort of thing.

In the 1950s, parents of children consigned to institutions in Pennsylvania got together and formed the Association for Retarded Children (the Arc) and began insisting that these children be provided services instead of just being warehoused. The movement for deinstitutionalization of children and adults with developmental disabilities was under way, and it continues today, having succeeded in closing most large-scale institutions all across the United States. As children were returned to their families, parents began to push for community-based services for these children. From closing institutions to unlocking the doors of public schools so that children with disabilities could be enrolled, parents have had a profound effect on the way society views these children and on the rights of people with disabilities to become full-fledged members of society.

Movement Toward Normalization

In the mid-1960s, parents again banded together with sympathetic professionals and pressed for the enactment of laws to provide services to people with disabilities. The civil rights movement of the 1950s and 1960s bolstered the parents' position, and in the late 1960s the principle known as "normalization" began to take hold. This essentially means that children and adults with developmental disabilities have a right to as normal a life as possible—similar to the lives of the rest of us—with access to education, friends, leisure activities, and work, and the joys and tears of daily life in the community.

In 1973, two federal laws were passed that changed the lives of people with developmental disabilities forever. One was the Rehabilitation Act of 1973, which extended civil rights protection to people with disabilities. This act stated that people with disabilities couldn't be discriminated against in terms of education, employment, transportation, and housing, from birth to death. (The Americans with Disabilities Act further extends these rights, as does the Developmental Disabilities and Bill of Rights Act.) The other law was the Education of All Handicapped Act of 1973 (since changed to the Individuals with Disabilities Education Act), which mandated the provision of a free, appropriate public education to all children with disabilities from age three through twenty-one. These laws helped people with disabilities move toward independence and self-determination. At last, children and adults with developmental disabilities were recognized as people of worth, people who could learn and grow and who had the same rights as any citizen of the United States.

My Journey with Susie

My daughter Susie was born in 1963. At the time, several people told my husband and I that we should consider institutionalizing her, but we felt very strongly that we wanted her to remain at home with us. Fortunately, we were not alone. Several other families in our area felt as we did, and we were able to get together occasionally to provide each other with emotional support.

Susie didn't start to walk until she was about two-and-a-half years old, and at five she was still barely talking and quite hyperactive. There was no preschool that would take Susie. She had no friends to play with, and several of our neighbors kept their children away. When it came time for kindergarten, there were no special education classes for her. It was only 1968, and the special education laws had not been written yet.

Because we had three older children attending our neighborhood school, and because we were active in the PTA, we were well known to the school staff. Mrs.

Tootel, a kindergarten teacher who had a child who was born deaf, volunteered to take Susie—no easy task with a class of twenty-seven other five-year-olds. The principal, Mr. Mial, was very supportive, as were several other teachers and several parents. Somehow or other, Susie stayed in kindergarten that year. When it was time for first grade, Mrs. Goldsmith, a first-grade teacher who had a daughter with learning disabilities, volunteered to take her. Again she was in a class with more than twenty other children.

The beautiful part of her kindergarten and first-grade placements was that the other children helped her and took pride in her accomplishments. They took their cues from the teachers, who were happy to have Susie in the class. In fact, several children in her class called me up one day to tell me that a *Cat in the Hat* special was on TV that night and to be sure that Susie watched it. (*The Cat in the Hat* was her favorite book.)

In September 1973, when Susie was nine-and-a-half years old, Michigan's Mandatory Special Education Act went into effect, and Susie finally had a place to go where they had to take her in, a special education class in our neighborhood public school. At last she was in a small class with a teacher specially trained to work with children like her. She still spent a little time in a few regular classes but was finally being taught at her own pace for the most part. Today, of course, children like Susie spend most of their time in a regular class with enough support provided for both them and their teachers so that they can participate fully.

Times Are Changing

When I was shopping with Susie a while ago, a woman with two young children in tow came over to us and exclaimed, "Is it? It is! Susie Greenbaum, I wondered what happened to you! How are you? Remember me? I'm Cora. You were in my second-grade class at Northside School." The woman turned to me and said, "I've been wondering where Susie was. I taught her to read when we were in Mrs. Street's class." She turned back to Susie and said, "Susie, this is my son, DJ, and my daughter, Cissy," and then she turned to her children and said, "This is Susie Greenbaum, she was in my class when I was your age." This interchange couldn't have happened thirty years ago, before laws went into effect mandating that children with disabilities had the right to attend public schools alongside their nondisabled neighbors.

Today

Since the early 1970s, many laws have been passed that provide services and supports for people with developmental disabilities. The parents of today's children with developmental disabilities look much less anxious than the parents of thirty years ago—largely thanks to these services and supports. Children with disabilities can receive services from birth, relieving their parents of a good deal of anxiety and uncertainty. There are training programs to help parents learn to care for and work with their children in ways that will help these children achieve their maximum potential. The more support available to a family with a child who has developmental disabilities, the less stress on the family and the more the family will be able to maintain a "normal" life.

Today people are much more accepting of children and adults with disabilities than they were fifty years ago. These children attend local schools with their neighbors, and teachers have learned a tremendous amount about how to educate them. These children are making more progress than we ever dreamed possible.

Education has opened doors. For example, children with Down syndrome, who were once considered severely retarded, today often function in the normal or near-normal range in school and later in life. It has become commonplace to see young adults with disabilities working in supermarkets and fast-food restaurants.

In 1930, the life expectancy of a child with developmental disabilities was only nineteen years. Today the life expectancy of these children is around sixty-six years, which means that most of them will outlive their parents. Of course, a large part of this increase in life expectancy is due to medical advances. But I believe that another major reason people with developmental disabilities are living longer is because they're now growing up surrounded by family and friends instead of being sent away to live in large institutions, away from the love of their family members, and away from the public eye.

Impacts on Parents and Families

The parents and families of people with developmental disabilities are as varied as the general population: rich and poor, highly educated and high-school dropouts, Democrats and Republicans—anyone may find themselves in this situation. Developmental disability is an equal-opportunity employer.

Much has been written about the feelings parents may experience on the birth of a child with disabilities. But researchers are only now beginning to examine parents' feelings as their child grows through adolescence and adulthood. If your child requires physical assistance, this becomes harder as he or she grows to adulthood, especially since you're getting older at the same time. And oftentimes, many of the rites of passage parents anticipate for their children simply don't occur for those with developmental disabilities; even when they do, days that are usually celebrated are often tinged with sadness or concern.

Parenting the Adolescent

The stress of having a child with developmental disabilities ebbs and flows. Some stages in the child's life are easier and others more difficult. Problems flare up at adolescence, when the differences between the child with developmental disabilities and nondisabled children widen. At a time when being liked by everyone else is a top priority, the adolescent with developmental disabilities may become socially isolated from the mainstream. On the other hand, as these children move through adolescence into adulthood, their families tend to become closer and more supportive of one another.

Missed Milestones of Adolescence

Milestones achieved by other children in the family or by friends' children—going off to college, for example—serve to point up the differences. And our sons and daughters probably notice the differences, too, even if they are mentally retarded or cognitively impaired. They want to graduate from high school and receive a diploma alongside their classmates even though they may not have mastered some very basic skills.

Letting go of a son or daughter with developmental disabilities who wants to go away to college or live on his or her own can be quite difficult for parents. For example, a person with severe autism has difficulty reading social cues or understanding others' feelings and thus may not be accepted by others or may get into situations he or she can't handle. If you have a child with severe cerebral palsy, whose support system you've been in charge of until now, you may worry that he or she won't be able to find the necessary supports away from home.

If you live in a small town where every teenager is driving, your teen may want to drive too. Trying to explain why he or she can't can be heartbreaking for both you and your child. However, don't automatically say no to driving unless legal issues are involved. Although some states won't issue licenses to people who are deaf or who have epilepsy, people who have a mental impairment can drive if they can pass both the written test and the road test. And adaptive controls on cars can enable many adults with physical disabilities to drive safely.

As your child reaches adolescence and grows into an adult, dating and romantic relationships may be a difficult issue—for your child and for you. You probably suffer every rejection and exclusion with him or her. It's important to keep your perspective and make every effort to ensure that your son or daughter interacts with adolescents of both sexes in as natural a way as possible. You must also ensure that he or she understands the responsibilities that go with relationships between teenage boys and girls.

When Susie was about thirteen years old, she turned to me one day and said "boy." I had no idea what she meant. She said "boy" again and pointed to herself. I still didn't understand. But when Susie said "boy" and pointed to herself the next time her older sister went out on a date, I finally understood what she meant. I asked her if she wanted to have a boyfriend. She eagerly said yes.

With the encouragement of my older children, I called a friend with a son, Jack, who also had developmental disabilities and explained the situation to her. We agreed to plan a "date" for the two of them at her house. On the appointed day, I brought Susie over, along with soda and cookies, and Susie and her "boy" adjourned to Jack's room (with the door open), turned on the tape recorder, and danced a bit. Within a few minutes they both emerged, happy with their date, and soon we went home.

For years afterward, Susie referred to "my boy Jack" whenever her older sister and brothers went out on dates.

Through the years Susie has had several "boyfriends" (she blushes whenever anyone refers to the young men as that). They hug each other when they meet and seem to enjoy each other's company, and they ask for nothing more from the relationship. One of the bonuses of living in a larger residential situation, as Susie does now, is that she can socialize with both males and females in a more normal setting.

Effects on Parents

Adolescents and young adults who have limited mobility can place quite a physical burden on parents who must feed, dress, and bathe them—just because of their size. A parent of a fifteen-year-old son with severe cerebral palsy probably must lift him at least five times to get him ready for breakfast. It's hard for outsiders to comprehend how much time a parent must put in on a daily basis for routine self-care tasks such as toothbrushing, combing hair, buttoning and zipping clothing, washing hands and face, even for an adolescent who is not obviously physically handicapped. Many parents have had to turn down promotions, change jobs, or cut back on their hours in order to care for a child with disabilities.

Finding sitters or professional caregivers for the adolescent or young adult with developmental disabilities can also be a challenge. It's usually hard to find someone both willing and able to sit with an adolescent or young adult who is mentally retarded or has severe physical disabilities.

Parenting the Adult

Based on my experience and that of the many other parents I've talked to, by the time these children become adults, they are usually relatively well integrated into their immediate families and pretty much accepted for who they are. They love and are loved by their brothers and sisters. They are loved by their grandparents, although sometimes not quite understood by them. And we parents are more often proud of their accomplishments than saddened by their limitations, which we've grown to accept. We have come to grips with many of the emotional issues of the adolescent and young adult period.

Missed Milestones of Early Adulthood

Although some adults with developmental disabilities get married and have children, most of them don't. If this causes you pain, it may help if you remind yourself that in this day and age not everyone has a long-term relationship, gets married, or has children. Alternative lifestyles can be very satisfactory for all sorts of people.

Moving out of the family home is another rite of passage your child has probably missed out on. Close to 75 percent of adults with developmental disabilities continue to live with their families (Fujiura and Park 2003), often because parents feel that the best place for their son or daughter is with the family. On the other hand, many parents would like to find another place for their adult child to live but don't know what their options are, or even that there are good alternatives to the family home.

Caretaking Continues

Adults with developmental disabilities still depend largely on their family for opportunities to socialize, even though they may be living and even working in the community. Although the general public may accept people with disabilities as neighbors and coworkers, they're far less likely to socialize with them. Unless your son or daughter gets together occasionally with other people with disabilities, he or she may be socially isolated.

Parents often must continue to assist adult sons or daughters with such things as eating, bathing, dressing, managing medications, and transportation, to name but a few daily activities. A small percentage of adults with developmental disabilities need constant surveillance for safety reasons. But generally speaking, most parents caring for an adult child with developmental disabilities tend to cope well with their responsibilities. Ongoing physical care of an adult with developmental disabilities does, however, begin to take its toll, especially as parents get older and their strength starts to wane. It's shocking to think that close to a million adults with developmental disabilities are cared for by parents sixty years of age and older (Fujiura and Park 2003).

Many parents are unaware of support services that can be immensely helpful, both to them and to their son or daughter. Or if they are aware of these services, they don't know how to access them (McCallion and Kolomer 2003). As a result, most adults with developmental disabilities aren't receiving the services to which they're entitled. Instead, they remain at home, growing increasingly lonely and bored, and their parents are very concerned. The amount of stress parents experience is largely dependent on the amount of support services the family receives.

We don't suffer from empty-nest syndrome, as other parents in their forties, fifties, and sixties do, because our nest is never quite empty. Our children with developmental disabilities are never far from our thoughts, even if they aren't living in our home. Many of us don't take vacations longer than two or three days because our sons and daughters might need us, even if they aren't living at home.

As we near retirement age, we begin to realize anew how different we are from other families. Many of us don't have enough money to retire, due to the financial drain that having a child with developmental disabilities can entail. And even if we do have some money and want to use it to travel or move to a warmer climate, we often don't because we feel we must be nearby to monitor the supports and services our sons and daughters are receiving. Sometimes, as we grow older, we parents become even more socially isolated—perhaps because we are just too tired to socialize or maybe because we feel we have little in common with people not in our situation.

On the other hand, parents who are caring for an adult child with developmental disabilities often say that caregiving can be very rewarding. They feel useful and needed. They're proud of what they do. In addition, they often feel that their son or daughter provides them with loving companionship as they get older. One parent reported how wonderful it is to see her daughter wake up each morning eager for the day to begin.

Research shows that parenting an adult with developmental disabilities can be a rewarding experience (McCallion and Kolomer 2003; Hayden and Heller 1997; Hartley and MacLean 2005). Parents and other family members of people with developmental disabilities generally say they appreciate life more and don't let small annoyances bother them (Dykens 2005). Siblings say they feel they have become more accepting of individual differences and have more patience and empathy for others. These siblings tend to be more altruistic than the general population. Many parents and siblings of individuals with developmental disabilities enter the helping professions, for example, becoming special education teachers, teacher's aides, or legal aid lawyers, or volunteering to work with poor or immigrant children.

Changing Roles in the Family

Now that your child with developmental disabilities has become an adult, it's likely that his or her siblings have, too. They may have gotten married and had children of their own, so you may now be a grandparent, and your adult child may be an uncle or aunt. As your other adult children embark on their own family lives, this may point up, once again, missed milestones. You may ache for your child with developmental disabilities, thinking he or she won't experience the joys of marriage—even though he or she may not be unhappy at all.

Through the years, you may have worried off and on about the effect on your other children of having a sibling with developmental disabilities. And now you may worry whether anyone will want to marry one of your other children if they find out they have a sibling with developmental disabilities. This worry can be laid to rest by examining the reality. Your other children can and will get married if they want to. They can and do find sympathetic spouses. You may worry about meeting your future in-laws and how they'll relate to your adult child. How will they feel about having a person with disabilities as a member of their extended family? Like the rest of society, some understand and some don't.

When my second son, Josh, got married, he insisted that Susie be an integral part of the wedding ceremony (and she decided to stand right up there with the bride and groom during the ceremony!). When I first met Josh's future in-laws, they said that they had never met a person who was retarded and weren't quite sure what to say or how to act. But at the wedding reception, when the bride and groom and parents of the bride and groom were invited out onto the dance floor for the first dance, Josh's new in-laws opened their arms wide and invited Susie to be part of their dance twosome. Because they live far away, they've rarely seen Susie since, but that was a precious moment in my life I will never forget.

Several of my first cousins are particularly close to Susie. On the other hand, several other family members really don't understand Susie and hardly consider her as part of their family. They make assumptions about her that aren't borne out by reality and make no attempt to inform themselves. You win some and you lose some. The parents I've interviewed report similar responses.

Becoming an in-law isn't such a stretch for an adult with developmental disabilities, but becoming an aunt or an uncle is quite a new role. Susie became an aunt when she was twenty. I'm not sure how much she really understood about the relationship at first. She knew that Wendy was her sister's baby. We all love babies, so Susie loved the baby. She called her "Baby Wendy" (and for a long time, she called each subsequent baby in the family "Baby Wendy"). We let her hold the baby, though we were always nearby to lend a hand if need be. Susie really enjoyed holding the baby and often asked us if she could.

Wendy grew up loving Susie because the rest of the family did. Many parents report that their adult child with developmental disabilities has different relationships with different nieces and nephews. Some they are close to; some they aren't. A young niece or nephew may not want to spend time with an aunt or uncle who is developmentally disabled. "She drools," one nephew said with disgust when he was five or six years old. "I don't want to sit next to her." Yet another niece or nephew may be exceedingly kind and loving.

Often nieces and nephews begin watching out for their aunt or uncle with developmental disabilities—without anyone asking them to. For example, a ten-year-old might remind her forty-year-old aunt not to answer the door when she's alone in the house. My granddaughter Wendy, who is now twenty-three, recently said to me "Grandma, I just want you to know that I will always look after Susie." I don't know how Wendy knew I was thinking about this.

Who Will Look After Your Child When You're Gone?

As all parents of children and adults with developmental disabilities will attest, their biggest concern is what will become of their son or daughter. Starting from the moment you find out that your child has developmental disabilities, this concern is always present at some level. This concern is easily understood in regard to those who are the most severely disabled: the daughter who can barely communicate her needs and the son who's entirely dependent on others for self-care. However, parents also worry about a son who may be only mildly disabled but can't relate to other people or is unable to become financially independent.

This concern starts edging to the forefront as parents get older and begin to worry about their continuing capability to care for their adult child. And this worry is well founded, because these days there is a strong likelihood that adults with developmental disabilities will outlive their parents. It's important for parents to realize that they aren't alone as they begin to seriously think about the future. There are community support services, not just for adults with developmental disabilities but for their families as well. These services include respite care, emergency services, residential services, financial support, and vocational training and placement.

More than half of the parents of people with developmental disabilities haven't made plans for their child's future. Yet good planning is critical: it can allay many of your fears about the future, and it can help your adult child with developmental disabilities lead a satisfying life, both now and after you're gone.

Getting to Know Maria, CJ, Susie, and Scott

In addition to my daughter Susie, Maria, CJ, and Scott are some of the adults with developmental disabilities you'll meet in this book. All of them have some degree of mental impairment, and several have physical impairments. Their parents are in various stages of thinking about the future. Scott's parents have already found a wonderful place for him to live, and he moved in this past year. CJ is living at home, an arrangement that works well because both he and his parents are happy with the situation. He contributes to the household by helping his mother in her business—cleaning houses. Maria's parents are in the midst of the planning process. Although they may decide that Maria's current residential situation is the best place for her, they want to explore other options in the community. I've already begun planning for Susie's future, but I have a long way to go.

Maria

Maria is a small, fair-haired young woman who wears thick glasses because she's legally blind. She dresses simply and has a good fashion sense; she takes after her stepmother in this regard. Like many people with developmental disabilities, Maria has a combination of disabilities: In addition to severely impaired eyesight, she has mild intellectual disabilities (mental retardation) and autism. Maria is generally quiet, although polite and friendly. She always greets visitors and tells them all the things she's done recently. Like many people with autism, Maria can recite dates, places, and encounters with people going back many years.

Maria functions well when she follows prescribed routines. For example, she can take an airplane by herself if she doesn't have to change planes. She knows what to do in case of a fire, but she can't sense if a situation is dangerous or if someone is menacing her. Her developmental disabilities, taken together, might be considered moderate.

CJ

CJ is a short, solidly built young man. He currently sports a buzz cut. A careful and meticulous worker, he has a good job working with his mother cleaning houses. He knows the routine cold and needs little or no direction to do his job well.

CJ has some health problems, and he really loses his temper occasionally. Although his speech can be hard to understand at times, he has an excellent vocabulary and a great sense of humor. Like many other people with Down syndrome, CJ has far exceeded expectations. When he was born, his parents were devastated and held out little hope for his future. Yet today, CJ might be considered to have only mild developmental disabilities.

Susie

My daughter Susie is a tall, pretty brunette who appears younger than she is, despite the fact that she has more than a few gray hairs. She leads a rich emotional life: She's often enthusiastic and happy, yet she's often frustrated and anxious, too.

Susie has limited speech and has difficulty with many self-care skills, such as washing her hair, brushing her teeth, and knowing what clothes to wear depending on the weather. She needs constant oversight because she might accidentally set fire to the kitchen when trying to make popcorn by herself. She has balance problems and walks with a somewhat jerky gait, and she's fearful of falling on snow and ice and other shiny surfaces. Many people assume that adults with moderate to severe developmental disabilities, like my daughter Susie, understand very little of the world around them. Yet as you'll see throughout the book, this is far from the case.

Scott

Scott is a small, good-looking young man with dark hair and dark eyes. There is a look of mischief about him. He has severe cerebral palsy with quadriplegia. In his case, that means he has little voluntary movement and great difficulty speaking. He also has some intellectual disabilities, but he is, essentially, untestable. Scott has enough voluntary movement in his left arm and hand to control an electric wheelchair.

Scott needs help with eating, bathing, dressing, and essentially all self-care skills. Since he has little control over his bladder and bowels, he must wear a condom catheter during the day when he's at school. He's still in school at age twenty-four because Michigan's special education law allows students with disabilities to attend school until their twenty-sixth birthday.

It's important to remember that people like Maria, CJ, Susie, and Scott have many abilities as well as disabilities, especially because any long-term plan for their future must address interests and strengths as well as needs. Maria plays the recorder and has a repertoire of close to fifty songs. She often plays at church during Sunday services. CJ is an excellent and methodical worker and can do his job with little supervision. He keeps up with all the latest sports news and might make a good color commentator on a sports program. Susie's major strength is that she is a caring and concerned friend who is in tune with other people's feelings. Scott loves Broadway musicals and can hum several tunes from his favorite shows.

Next Steps

Perhaps you're reading this book to check on what you're doing and possibly make a few changes or modifications to your current situation. Or perhaps you're ready to begin the complicated process of planning for the future. Whatever your reason, it's important to take stock of your child's current situation and, with his or her input, improve it where you can. Knowing what is and isn't working now is also critical information for planning for the future. It's also important to examine your own quality of life to see if it could be improved or enhanced. Keeping your strength up and nurturing your optimism are necessary prerequisites for caring for your adult child and making well-thought-out plans for the future.

In the next chapter, you'll assess your current situation and find out how satisfied you are with the way you're living your life. You'll do the same for your son or daughter. Then, in chapters 3 and 4, you'll find suggestions for fine-tuning various aspects of life, both yours and your child's, without making any major changes in where your child is living.

CHAPTER 2

Taking Inventory

Any parent's sense of well-being is inextricably tied up with their children's well-being, although the more independent one's children are, the looser the tie. The tie is particularly tight when you have an adult child with developmental disabilities. This is true regardless of where or with whom your child lives. You probably think about your son or daughter almost all the time and worry about whether he or she is safe and happy.

There's actually a reciprocal relationship between parents' sense of well-being and that of their children. If you feel good, your child is more likely to feel good. And if your child feels good, you're more likely to feel good.

Although parents of adults with developmental disabilities generally cope quite well, we do have a lot more responsibility—and work—than other parents. And we generally have a lot more on our minds. For this very reason, it's important to set aside some time to sit back and take a look at how things are going, both for you and for your child.

The assessments below will help you determine which parts of your life are satisfactory, which you aren't happy with and would like to change, and which things in your life just need a little fine-tuning to make them acceptable. It's important to take the right approach when assessing your child's current situation. Most of us monitor our sons' and daughters' life situation fairly often, asking ourselves, "Is he happy?" "Is she watching television too much?" "Are they giving him his medication?" But we don't do this in a systematic way, and we may not try very hard to find out how our children feel about their situation.

See the Situation from Your Son's or Daughter's Point of View

Recently our community agency offered to move Susie from the large (fifty-resident) church-run center at the edge of town where she was living into a small group home in the community. The decision was a difficult one. As I wavered back and forth in my decision, I finally told myself to try to see it from Susie's point of view. There are many advantages to living in the community, and participation in community activities is a big one. Susie loved going to our neighborhood school when she was a child, and when she's visiting me she likes to go outside to talk to the neighbors or the mail carrier. She likes to go shopping and to the farmers' market. So I imagined she would probably enjoy living in town, surrounded by people and cars and stores.

Although her current situation wasn't perfect, she loved her direct care worker very much and would miss her terribly if she left. She enjoyed being able to go by herself to visit other friends at the center or to visit favorite staff members. And she particularly loved her work activity program, which she would have to leave if she moved.

In both living situations, Susie could go shopping, bowling, to a movie, and to a restaurant several times a week. If Susie moved to the small group home, she would miss being able to go outside by herself, without a direct care worker, and her day-to-day circle of friends would be limited to the three to six residents of the group home and one staff member. As I weighed the pros and cons from Susie's point of view, my decision became clear. I believed Susie would want to stay where she was.

When assessing your child's current situation, try to ensure that the answers to the questions are those he or she would give. You may be surprised to discover that in some cases you and your child might answer a question differently.

Completing the Assessments

In order to make any changes or improvements in your life or your child's life, it's important to find out where you and your adult child are now. In the first assessment, we'll look at your situation; for example, you'll record how much time you are currently devoting to your adult child with developmental disabilities and how much time you're able to devote to your other needs and interests. In the second assessment, we'll look at your child's current living situation, activities, social life, health, and general life situation. Be sure to date both worksheets. When life is stressful, it can be hard to remember what happened when or to gauge your progress. Once you've filled out the assessments, you can look back at them at any time to see where you were and how you're progressing.

ASSESS YOUR CURRENT SITUATION

Answer all of the questions below. Where appropriate, circle the answers that best describe your situation and feelings, and explain your answers where indicated. If you need more space than is provided, just use a separate sheet of paper. Or you may wish to keep a special journal as you work through this book, using it both for exercises such as this one and to capture any thoughts, feelings, or ideas that come up during the process.

How old are you? _____ Date: _____

How many people live in your home? _____

Who are they? _____

_____

Do you have any chronic health problems? Yes No

If yes, please describe: _____

_____

Does your spouse or partner have any chronic health problems? Yes No

If yes, please describe: _____

_____

How much of the time does your son or daughter live at home with you?

_____ All of the time _____ Most of the time
_____ Some of the time _____ Just for visits

Are you happy with this arrangement? Yes No

Is your spouse or partner happy with this situation? Yes No

Are your other children happy with this situation? Yes No

Why do they feel this way? _____

_____

Do you feel that this situation is the best one for your son or daughter? Yes No

Explain your answer: _____

_____

Would you like your son or daughter to live elsewhere, if you could find a good place for him or her? Yes No

If yes, where? _____

Where do you expect your son or daughter to live when you are no longer able to take care of him or her? _____

Do you feel you are spending enough time with your spouse and other children? Yes No

If no, please explain: _____

_____

Are you generally satisfied with your family life? Yes No

If no, please explain: _____

_____

Work and Volunteer Activities

Are you working outside the home? Yes No

Number of hours: _____

Are you generally satisfied with your job? Yes No

Would you prefer to work someplace else? Yes No

If yes, where? _____

If you aren't working outside the home, would you prefer to work? Yes No

If yes, where? _____

Do you do volunteer work? Yes No

Are you generally satisfied with your volunteer activities? Yes No

Leisure

Are you taking any classes? Yes No

If yes, please describe: _____

Do you participate in community activities? Yes No

If yes, please describe: _____

Do you have any hobbies? Yes No

If yes, please describe: _____

How often do you take vacations?

_____ Never _____ Rarely _____ Sometimes _____ Often

How often do you attend religious services?

_____ Never _____ Rarely _____ Sometimes _____ Often

What other leisure activities do you participate in? _____

_____

Are you happy with the amount of time you spend on leisure activities? Yes No

Social Life

How often do you visit friends?

_____ Never _____ Rarely _____ Sometimes _____ Often

How often do you invite friends to visit you?

_____ Never _____ Rarely _____ Sometimes _____ Often

How often do you see extended family members?

_____ Never _____ Rarely _____ Sometimes _____ Often

How is your social life?

_____ Satisfactory _____ So-so _____ Unsatisfactory

Caring for Your Son or Daughter

When your son or daughter is home, how much time do you spend physically caring for him or her on a daily basis?

_____ Less than one hour _____ One to two hours _____ More than two hours

Describe the care you provide: _____

_____

_____

_____

How much time do you spend guiding or supervising your son or daughter on a daily basis?

_____ Rarely needs supervision
_____ Needs supervision about half the time
_____ Needs constant supervision

Does someone else take care of your son or daughter on a regular basis? Yes No

How frequently?

_____ Daily _____ Once or twice a week
_____ Once a month _____ Rarely _____ Never

Do you ever feel that the care of your son or daughter is becoming too much for you? Yes No

In either case, please explain: _____

_____

How frequently do you worry about your son or daughter?

_____ All the time _____ Often _____ Seldom

What do you worry about? _____

_____

What do you do if caregiving becomes too draining, emotionally or physically? _____

_____

_____

Your Quality of Life

In general, how would you describe the quality of your life at this time?

_____ Very good _____ Fairly good _____ Neither good nor bad
_____ Not very good _____ Not good at all

How would you describe your child's quality of life at this time?

_____ Very good _____ Fairly good _____ Neither good nor bad
_____ Not very good _____ Not good at all

How do you feel most of the time? (circle all that apply)

Safe	Hopeful	Capable	Exhausted
Contented	Lonely	Empty	Brave
Respected	Anxious	Stressed-out	Fulfilled
Angry	Valuable	Depressed	Satisfied
Friendly	Afraid	On top of things	Bitter

Change

Are there some things about your life you would like to see changed or modified? Yes No

If yes, please describe: _____

_____

Are there some things about your child's life you would like to see changed or modified? Yes No

If yes, please describe: _____

_____

Have you made plans for your child's future? Yes No

If yes, please describe: _____

_____

_____

ASSESS YOUR CHILD'S CURRENT SITUATION

If your son or daughter with developmental disabilities can't understand the following questions or has difficulty answering, you may have to translate the questions into words he or she can understand, and you may have to translate his or her responses as well. It may even be that you have to provide answers, taking his or her point of view as best as you can. If he or she can't answer verbally, try observing his or her behavior for a few days and then writing down your best guess of his or her feelings and opinions.

Date: _____

How old is your son or daughter? _____

Residential Situation

Where is your son or daughter currently living?

_____ With you

_____ With another family member

_____ Alone

_____ In an apartment or house with one to four others (nonfamily)

_____ In a group home (with six to fifteen others)

_____ In a residence with more than fifteen and less than fifty others

_____ In a residence with more than fifty others

_____ Other: _____

Is your child's present living situation relatively permanent? Yes No

Is your child's present living situation satisfactory to him or her? Yes No

What does he or she like about it? _____

_____

_____

What does he or she dislike about it? _____

_____

_____

Would he or she like to change it? Yes No

Where would he or she like to live? _____

_____

Who would he or she like to live with? _____

_____

Activities

Is your son or daughter working? Yes No

If so, how many hours per week? _____

Describe the work situation: _____

_____

_____

Is he or she satisfied with the work situation? Yes No

In either case, please explain: _____

_____

_____

If he or she isn't working, would he or she like to work? Yes No

Does he or she go to a sheltered workshop or day activity center for people with disabilities? Yes No

If so, describe the activities at the workshop or center: _____

_____

Is he or she satisfied with the sheltered workshop or day activity center? Yes No

In either case, please explain: _____

_____

_____

Is he or she involved in any volunteer activities? Yes No

If so, please describe: _____

_____

Is he or she involved in community activities? Yes No

If so, please describe: _____

_____

Would he or she like to participate in more community activities? Yes No

If yes, please describe: _____

_____

Does he or she do any chores around the house, such as food prep or cleaning?
Yes No

If yes, please describe: _____

_____

Describe your child's typical day: _____

_____

_____

Social Life

How often does your son or daughter see friends?

_____ Never _____ Rarely _____ Sometimes _____ Often

How often does he or she see members of the extended family?

_____ Never _____ Rarely _____ Sometimes _____ Often

How often does he or she go out to eat or to a movie?

_____ Never _____ Rarely _____ Sometimes _____ Often

How often does he or she participate in sports?

_____ Never _____ Rarely _____ Sometimes _____ Often

What other social activities does he or she participate in? _____

_____

Is your child satisfied with his or her social life? Yes No

If no, why not? _____

_____

Health

Does your child have a chronic health condition? Yes No

If yes, please describe: _____

_____

Is he or she overweight? Yes No

Does he or she get some daily exercise? Yes No

If yes, please describe: _____

_____

Does he or she spend some time outdoors most days? Yes No

Professional Caregivers

Which of your child's professional caregivers does he or she like? _____

_____

Why? _____

_____

Which of your child's professional caregivers does he or she dislike? _____

_____

Why? _____

_____

Quality of Life

How does your son or daughter feel most of the time? Please circle all that apply.

Safe	Hopeful	Capable	Overwhelmed
Contented	Lonely	Enthusiastic	Frustrated

Relaxed	Respected	Anxious	Satisfied	Fulfilled
Angry	Valuable	Depressed	Stressed-out	
Friendly	Fearful	Well cared for		

Other: _____

What are the three most important things in your child's life at this time?

1. _____

2. _____

3. _____

In general, how does your child feel about his or her quality of life at this time?

_____ Very good _____ Fairly good _____ Neither good nor bad
_____ Not very good _____ Not good at all

Change

Are there things your child would like to see changed or modified about his or her life? Yes No

If yes, please describe: _____

_____

_____

Fine-Tuning the Current Situation

After assessing your current situation, you may feel that it's satisfactory and that no change is necessary. That would be great. In an ideal world, the same would be true for your son's or daughter's current situation. However, given the challenges both of you face, it's likely that at least a few things need adjustment. Sometimes minor modifications can transform a somewhat unsatisfactory situation into a satisfactory one. Or you may want to make more substantial changes to the current situation, such as adding respite care for a son or daughter living in your home or getting a part-time job for yourself that you enjoy and that contributes to your sense of well-being.

If you think it would be best to change where your adult child lives, and with whom, this is a major change that requires careful long-term planning. Before making such major changes or coming up with a long-term plan, first make the current situation as satisfactory as possible. This will enable you to take the time you need to develop a well-thought-out plan for the future and move toward its fulfillment.

Next Steps

Save your answers to these questionnaires and look back over them from time to time. If you answered most of the questions in a positive manner, you can justifiably feel pleased that you've been able to build a life for yourself and your adult child that brings you satisfaction. This book will help you use the positives in your life to plan for the future.

Don't be discouraged if you answered some of these questions negatively. Your situation is difficult, and it would be surprising if there were nothing that you'd like to change or improve. This book will help you turn those difficult answers into tools for developing a satisfactory life for yourself as well as for your son or daughter. Chapter 3 will discuss ways you can enhance your own quality of life in light of your answers to these questionnaires, and in chapter 4 we'll do the same for your adult child with developmental disabilities.

CHAPTER 3

Making the Most of Your Current Situation

Most parents of adults with developmental disabilities cope quite well with their responsibilities for their son or daughter—a large part of the time (Chen et al. 2001; Seltzer and Krauss 2002; Dykens 2005). But a review of the research on parents in our situation reveals that we often function under a great deal of physical and mental stress.

Our lives may be less well-rounded or fulfilling, due to missed career opportunities. Many parents (especially mothers) have either passed up job opportunities or cut back on the number of hours they work, or they've quit their jobs entirely in order to take care of their child with developmental disabilities. We parents have difficulty finding time for recreation and socializing. And often we find ourselves too tired to have fun (Heller, Hsieh, and Rowitz 1997).

The purpose of this chapter is to help relieve some of your stress and make your life a little easier. You'll learn ways to help you brighten your outlook and enrich your life. You've probably gotten very good at taking care of others, and you may feel that you can't take time from this important task to take care of yourself. But remember, you need to take care of yourself so that you'll continue to have the strength and energy to help care for your adult child with developmental disabilities.

Take Care of Yourself

All of us need to take care of ourselves. You may wish that others would step forward to take care of you, but you're the best person for the job because you know yourself best. You know your needs. You know what would ease your mind and heart. Sometimes loving family or friends may guess what it is you want or what will help you. But chances are they, like you, find themselves pressed for time and in need of a little self-care themselves!

Human beings have a limited supply of strength and stamina, and you've probably been using up yours at an alarming rate. Parenting an adult with developmental disabilities is a demanding task. Many of us are aging, and time may be taking its toll. You may be wiser, but you're probably also more tired.

If you've ever ridden in an airplane, no doubt you'll recall that the safety instructions tell you to put on your own oxygen mask before putting on your child's. Why? So that you can remain functional and alert in order to help your child. Remind yourself of this whenever you worry about taking time away from your son or daughter to do something for yourself.

There are other benefits to taking good care of yourself. You'll have more zest to devote to your important relationships. You'll have more love to devote to your family. And you'll live a longer and happier life. Although there's no need to justify that benefit, it does mean that you'll be around longer to advocate for and assist your adult child.

The Eight Rs for Parents of Adults with Developmental Disabilities

The increasing incidence of Alzheimer's disease has focused a spotlight on family caregivers. The media have devoted a great deal of coverage to the issue, and support groups for family members have sprung up all over the country. As a society, we're beginning to realize that most caregivers get worn out over a period of time, whether caring for a loved one with Alzheimer's or a loved one with developmental disabilities. And you, as the parent of an adult with developmental disabilities, have been a caregiver longer than most.

You need a break or a breather at least occasionally, if not frequently. The following eight Rs are ways you can refresh yourself:

1. Reassess your situation.

2. Renew yourself.

3. Redefine yourself.

4. (Take a) respite from your responsibilities.

5. Relax.

6. Reassure yourself.

7. Reinforce your family ties.

8. Reward yourself.

All of them will help you refresh yourself and regroup, so you'll have renewed energy to deal with the responsibilities of caregiving.

Reassess Your Situation

We often fall into habits and routines that no longer serve us well. For example, maybe you still take the same old route to the mall even though a new and better road has recently been built. Times change and new services become available. Social services personnel we may not have liked or trusted move on. And, thankfully, new laws are passed that grant more rights and benefits to people with developmental disabilities and their families. It's important to reassess your life occasionally in light of these changes, to see if what you're doing still serves you best.

Look back at the exercise in chapter 2 in which you took stock of your current situation and assessed your life, then answer the questions below:

In general, is your life satisfactory? Yes No

Could it be better? Yes No

How? _____

_____

_____

Use your answer to this question as a signpost pointing out directions you must go in order to make your life richer and more rewarding. The remaining seven Rs will help you get where you want to go.

Renew Yourself

Do you ever feel that most of the love and caring in your life is flowing outward from you to others? You need to take in some love and support to replenish your supply. There are many avenues to finding the caring and support you need to continue functioning well: Look within yourself, look to your friendships and your faith, and don't rule out options like support groups and therapy.

Become Your Own Best Friend

Sometimes you may be quite hard on yourself, saying such things to yourself as "Boy, that's dumb" or "I wish I were more patient" or "If I were a better parent, I could…." There's an all-too-human tendency to feel guilty about the things we haven't done instead of proud of the things we have done (Nichols 1996).

Becoming your own best friend means caring for yourself as your best friend would. Best friends are understanding and encouraging, help each other solve problems, do fun things together, give each other good advice, and sometimes present each other with wonderful gifts.

Think of what you would say to your best friend if he or she were feeling down. You'd want to help your friend feel better, and you would say things like "Stop being so critical of yourself" or "Stop feeling guilty for stealing a well-deserved moment or two for yourself" or "Don't feel ashamed if you get frustrated and angry sometimes; you're a better person than you give yourself credit for."

What are some other things your best friend might say to you if you were feeling down or stressed or anxious? Be specific. _____

_____

_____

_____

Really give some thought to this, and when you've come up with a few statements that seem helpful, consider making a list and keeping it with you. When you're upset or having a tough time, take out your list and try saying these things to yourself.

Nurture Your Friendships

Don't isolate yourself. Reach out to others. Your friends don't all have to understand what it's like to have an adult with disabilities in the family. Choose different friends to suit your different interests: Perhaps some of them will like the same books, others will like to play golf, and yet others will like the same kinds of music.

If you feel tired, you may see socializing as a chore. Don't let feeling tired get in the way. You'll find that social occasions can help you relax and enjoy yourself, and they may even revitalize you. Life often seems rosier after social occasions.

You may tell yourself that you're too busy to socialize. Make the time anyway (see "Take Respite," below, for suggestions). Make a list of your closest friends, and next to each, note when the last time was that you were in touch with or saw that person. It doesn't take much time to make a phone call, and it goes a long way toward maintaining a good friendship. Email is even easier. Make a pledge to yourself to contact at least one good friend this week.

Friends can help leaven our lives with laughter. As you work on the eight Rs and your interests outside the home expand, you'll have more opportunities to make new friends. Keep your eyes open.

Try Support Groups

Sometimes you need an understanding and sympathetic ear. Another parent who cares for an adult child with developmental disabilities will probably really understand when you say, "I just wanted to run out of the house and never come back!" These were the exact words a woman recently shared in an informal support group. A relative newcomer, she had rarely contributed anything to our rambling discussions, but she listened attentively. One day, however, she arrived late and looking rather disheveled. Suddenly she broke down and began to tell us how very difficult her life was, trying to do everything for everyone in her family and caring for an adolescent son with severe cerebral palsy. Of course we understood; we had all been there ourselves.

The emotional support of shared tears and hugs is invaluable, but there are practical benefits, too. The rest of us could offer suggestions from our own experience that might help, and one parent of an older son with cerebral palsy offered to help out one evening so the woman and her husband could go out for a night on the town. She didn't want to accept, but after we all urged her to, she relented. This was not the end of all her problems, of course. But she began to feel like a human being again and began thinking about how to make her life easier.

Because support groups are made up of parents like yourself, they can help you vent about some of your most difficult feelings and experiences without fear of correction or disapproval. They can help you feel that you're not alone, that you have people who understand you. And, importantly, support groups can provide you with respite, allowing you to add some relaxation and fun to your life. They can also provide you with information. For example, Scott's mother told me that one of the parents in her United Cerebral Palsy support group told her about condom catheters. No doctor had suggested this option to her. Up to that time Scott had been using indwelling catheters, which were quite uncomfortable for him.

What kinds of questions might you have for other parents in your situation?

_____

_____

What concerns do you have that only other parents in your situation might understand? _____

_____

_____

What success stories would you like to share with other parents? _____

_____

_____

_____

Community agencies often run support groups for parents and caregivers. These tend to be run by a professional and often include a presentation on an important topic as well as a discussion. They tend to be a bit more formal. Alternatively, you may hear of or want to start a more informal group, as ours was—a random group of parents, friends of friends, and acquaintances met in clinics or while standing in line at the grocery store. Whether formal or informal, support groups can help you over many a difficult patch.

There are many resources for finding out about ongoing support groups in your community. Whether you do your research by telephone or on the Internet, here are some places to start:

- Mental health agencies

- Hospitals

- The National Council on Aging (www.ncoa.org)

- The Arc (formerly the Association for Retarded Citizens; www.thearc.org)

- United Cerebral Palsy (www.ucp.org)

- In the yellow pages under Support Groups, Social Services, Community Agencies, or Human Services Organizations

- In the phone book in the county or city government pages

Consider Therapy

Sometimes the emotional support you get from parent support groups isn't enough, especially if you're seriously depressed for a period of time. Signs of depression include significant difficulty falling asleep at night, loss of appetite, pervasive sadness or hopelessness, suicidal thoughts, and periods of intense anxiety that continue over several weeks or more. If you think you may be depressed, it's important that you find a psychiatrist, psychologist, or social worker whom you can talk with about your situation. It's possible that medication or other interventions might help you over the hump.

You should also seek out a therapist if your family relationships are suffering. You can ask your family physician or your community mental health agency for a referral.

If you have a local chapter of the Arc or United Cerebral Palsy, they may also be able to provide recommendations, and they may know of therapists who have more experience with the types of issues you face.

Renew Your Faith

Many parents have found comfort in a church, synagogue, or other faith-based group. Sharing the fellowship of others and feeling that someone is watching over you can help you rest your burden and renew your strength.

Redefine Yourself

Many parents focus so much of their energy on their child with a disability that they lose themselves. They shelve their dreams and careers in order to focus on the here and now of caring for their son or daughter. As the parent of a child with a disability, you do face certain hurdles, but that doesn't mean that you should have a limited view of your future. This is just part of your life situation; it doesn't define who you are.

First of all, remind yourself of your talents and strong points. List them here:

_____

_____

_____

_____

Now list some of the things you've enjoyed doing in the past:

_____

_____

_____

_____

Say you wanted to be a dancer; it isn't too late to take a course at your local dance studio. Did you ever want to be a biochemist? Get a catalog from your local college and see what courses they have to offer. If you ever wanted to learn how to make pottery, take a ceramics class. If you didn't have responsibilities, and if you had enough time, what would you do? Take some time to think about this. Visualize yourself living one of your dreams. What do you see? _____

_____

_____

_____

How do you feel in this dream? _____

_____

Why does this dream appeal to you? _____

_____

Is there a part of your dream you can begin working on now? _____

_____

Or perhaps you've been toying with a new idea but rejected it because of your situation or because you don't think you have the time. Now is the time to consider how you might be able to make it happen. What is your idea or wish? ____

_____

What barriers do you see to attaining it? _____

_____

Brainstorm some ways you might overcome or bypass those barriers: _____

_____

_____

_____

Nurture your dreams. Begin to transform them into reality. Let them become a part of who you are. Start to work on something special—something just for yourself. Resurrect some old interests or develop new ones.

Don't be intimidated by the difficulties. It's okay to start small. To increase your involvement with the wider world, subscribe to a local or national newspaper and some interesting magazines. Go to the library or bookstore and get some new books. Commit to getting out of the house more often, and buy yourself some clothes that make you feel interesting and even sexy. Plan a date with your spouse or partner.

Perhaps you don't have any grand visions of your future or abandoned dreams you'd like to rekindle. That's fine; you can still redefine yourself simply by taking time to be in different surroundings and interacting with different people. You can plan to have lunch with a friend at a new restaurant in town, or you can take a long walk on a spring day. You can go to the gym, a movie, a lecture, or a casino. Anything that will remove the weight from your heart for a while will be good for you.

How to Find the Time

"But I don't have time," you say. "There's too much to do." But is it really lack of time, or have you just forgotten how to enjoy yourself, what with all your long-term worries and concerns? Surely there's some time in the day you can set aside for yourself. And if there isn't, you must find a way to make the time.

Finding time often means rearranging your priorities. Think of all the things you have to do in a day, prioritize them from most to least important, then drop those with a low priority. Be ruthless. Then make your personal time one of the two or three top priorities.

Here are some specific tips on how to find more time:

- Share your responsibilities with others in your household.

- Reorganize your daily routine.

- Hire someone to clean your house, at least occasionally.

- Order take-out dinners on occasion. You certainly don't have to cook every day.

- Arrange for someone to care for your son during your personal time. (See chapter 8, on caregivers).

List some ways you can find more time for yourself: _____

_____

_____

_____

But taking time for yourself isn't just a question of finding time in your day or week; you also need to find time in your head. You need to clear away all your worries and responsibilities for a brief time and focus only on yourself. One good way of doing this is to talk to yourself as your best friend would, reminding yourself that you're an attentive parent most of the time and that this is your time for yourself. Another way is through meditation. Meditation classes are offered in many places: community recreation centers, yoga institutes, Buddhist temples, wellness centers, the Y, and more.

By the way, I'm not just talking about a random hour here or there; I'm talking about finding blocks of time you can devote to yourself and the things you want to do on a regular basis. And when you do find or make the time, be sure to devote this time to yourself, not just to catching up on your other responsibilities.

Change Jobs or Start a New Career

Many parents of adults with developmental disabilities have either quit work or put their careers on hold. Yet research shows that being employed has a positive effect on the physical and mental health of parents of adults with developmental disabilities (Chen et al. 2001). One parent who had a part-time job that required all her attention when she was at work said that she got a vacation from her concerns every time she went to work.

Parents who quit their jobs feel they must give their all to their child and that they have little time left over to pursue a good job or career. They tend to define themselves in terms of their son or daughter, and their world is quite small. Don't get caught in this trap. Having a satisfying job goes a long way toward having a satisfying life, and a paycheck is a tangible symbol that someone thinks your efforts are worthwhile and valuable. When you're taking care of your child, you're bound to feel inept or discouraged sometimes. A satisfying job can reinforce your feeling of self-worth.

If you're not working, consider enriching your life by going back to work. Return to the career you had before you decided to devote your life to your child. Or start a new career: Become a teacher, administrator, bus driver, data-entry clerk, cook, gardener, or researcher—or start your own small business. It's never too late to start a career (Fellman 2000). Plenty of fifty-year-olds have gone back to college or gotten an advanced degree.

To help you brainstorm about what sort of job or career would work for you, answer the following questions:

What careers or jobs interest you? _____

_____

_____

What skills do you have? (These can be skills you learned in school or at work, including volunteer work, or skills you learned at home as a caregiver or homemaker.) _____

_____

_____

What further training do you need to learn the skills necessary for a particular job? (This may require some research on your part.) _____

_____

What jobs are available right now? (Talk to friends and acquaintances. Look through the help-wanted section in your local newspaper.) _____

_____

_____

There are quite a few good books that can help you make decisions about an appropriate and fulfilling job or a career. Search on Amazon.com using a term such as "job hunting," or visit your local bookstore.

You'll need training for some jobs, whereas others you can just walk right into. Consider taking a beginning or advanced computer class to prepare yourself. You might start by working just a few hours a day, so you don't feel overwhelmed. This will probably be an easier way to start, rather than rearranging your entire life to take a full-time job.

If you're unsure of your qualifications or feel your skills are rusty, consider volunteering for a while at your local hospital or church. Or work on a political campaign or get involved in a community agency that works with low-income families. Volunteering can be very rewarding and often leads to a paying job. Many local newspapers include a listing of volunteer activities.

List some volunteer jobs you might be interested in: _____

_____

_____

You can find the hours you need by arranging for either in-home or out-of-home respite care for your son or daughter. Respite, the next of the eight Rs, can help you find the time you need to renew and redefine yourself.

Take Respite

"Respite" means a short rest—from the care of your child and from other responsibilities as well. Respite care can give you the gift of time, allowing you to renew yourself: your physical and emotional strength, your love for yourself and others, and your enthusiasm for life. Respite is a necessity for you and your family—not an option—something I've had to learn over and over again.

Between Christmas and New Year's, and on occasional weekends during the year, my daughter Susie and her best friend, Maria, go to Camp Fowler, a camp for adolescents and adults with various disabilities. It's a real camp, complete with hayrides, bonfires, arts and crafts, and singing and dancing. Susie and Maria really look forward to going there—and Maria's parents and I look forward to it too. Those weekends the two friends attend camp are golden for us. We lay aside our worries and rest, relax, invite friends over, or take a quick trip. Camps like this are located across the country.

I also have a wonderful sitter, Penny, whom I've used through the years. Susie looks forward to seeing her, and truth be told, as much as Susie loves me and needs me, she also gets bored with me. Though it's difficult to admit, you may have found that your son or daughter gets bored with you, too.

Respite can give you a brief reprieve from the stresses of your difficult life and provide you with time to relax and do some of the things you've always wanted to. I cannot stress enough the importance of finding respite for yourself. Time away from daily care and worry is essential if you are to create a satisfying life for yourself and your child. Not only is respite good for you, it's also good for your son or daughter. It can provide him or her with change and stimulation—and relief from you! However, it's important to find someone you can trust to take good care of your son or daughter.

Respite Providers

Hopefully, you have someone in your life you can turn to right now: a family friend, a relative, a longtime sitter. If not, you can ask other parents who they use (one good reason to join a support group!). Sometimes the department of social services at a nearby hospital can give you a list of potential sitters. You can also hire nursing or education students from your local college or university; perhaps you can put an ad on their student bulletin boards.

If you are over age sixty and caring for an adult child with developmental disabilities, you can call your local Council on Aging (www.ncoa.org) to inquire about respite services. You may be able to locate them in your telephone directory in the city or county government pages.

If you worry that your son or daughter will be unhappy when you're out and about, ask yourself, "What are some things I do now with my child that a sitter or respite worker could do?" Familiar outings such as going shopping, taking a walk, or going to the movies are examples of activities a respite worker can do with your son or daughter, easing the transition for him or her.

Take the time now to list some activities your son or daughter could do with a respite worker that would be fun or provide a sense of continuity in familiar, enjoyable routines:

_____

_____

Various community agencies can provide respite services, and different types of respite services are available, depending on agency priorities and funding. (For more details on community agencies, see chapter 9). In-home respite is much like a traditional sitter arrangement, except that the respite care worker is required to interact with your son or daughter rather than watch TV. In out-of-home respite, you take your child to a place that provides respite care for several hours or several days.

Sometimes community agencies don't actually provide respite care workers but will pay for those you hire yourself. For example, the agency might give you a yearly stipend for respite care.

Respite services are particularly important during family emergencies, such as a parent's illness or a death in the family. In these cases, respite becomes a necessity. Fortunately, community agencies usually provide emergency respite care.

Go to your phone book and locate the phone numbers of community agencies in your area that may provide respite services. Look in the yellow pages under Social Services Agencies, Community Agencies, or Human Services Agencies, and also look in the state, county, and local government pages. When contacting these agencies, you must ask them if they provide respite services, since they provide many other services as well.

Write the names of the agencies and their phone numbers here so you'll have easy access to all of this information in one place: _____

_____

_____

The person who provides respite care need not do everything just the same or as well as you do, but he or she does need to do it responsibly and in accord with the safety and health needs of your child. You can write out lists for the respite care worker to ensure that he or she is clear on what needs to be done. If your child is medically or emotionally fragile and you're concerned about being out of touch when you're away from home, you can carry a cell phone with you so that you can be contacted if necessary.

If you've never used a caregiver from outside the family, the first few times can be scary. But after a while you'll find yourself relaxing and enjoying whatever you've chosen to do with this gift of time.

Relax

Relaxation is a state we constantly seek but rarely find. Many people will tell you to try to relax when faced with a challenging task. However, that's more easily said than done. This section will discuss some research-based techniques you can use to help you relax.

First, avoid as much stress as you can. This means avoiding stressful situations or people whenever it's practical or possible to do so. You can't avoid all stress, but you can avoid some stressors.

Second, talk to yourself. Tell yourself to relax. Tell yourself to count to the proverbial ten. Tell yourself to take it easy—"don't sweat the small stuff." And tell yourself to take a deep breath, and then do it. As simple as this technique is, it's amazingly effective. Try it next time you're feeling upset, tense, or worried.

Third, use visualization. Internal imagery is strongly linked to our emotions. You've probably experienced this firsthand when imagining an upsetting event—it can be quite stressful and even affect you physically. Luckily, it works the other way, too, and you can help yourself relax by visualizing yourself in a pleasant place, such as lying in a hammock on a beautiful sunny day listening to the water tumble in a nearby brook. You can visualize yourself in an idealized situation or in a situation you've already experienced in which you were relaxed. Remember how wonderful you felt in that situation.

Fourth, exercise regularly. Exercise releases endorphins, which help you relax and give you a sense of well-being. I found this out when I took up skiing at the grand old age of forty-five. It was difficult for me since I'm quite uncoordinated. But once I skied down my first little bunny hill, I was hooked. I went every week and really worked hard. Sometimes I felt too tired to go and wanted to stay home, but my friends insisted that I go. I soon found that no matter how tired I was before I started to ski, by the time I stopped I felt relaxed and happy.

Fifth, learn how to meditate. I once met a man who worked on an assembly line in a large automobile factory. He was required to work quickly and accurately in an extremely noisy environment. Boy, did he need to relax during his break! But there was really no place to go except outside into the small concrete storage yard, where a small scraggly tree had wedged itself into a corner. Having learned meditation in a class at his local Y, he chose to sit beneath that scraggly tree, close his eyes, and meditate for fifteen to twenty minutes during his break. When he went back to work, he felt immensely rested and relaxed—it was better than taking a nap. He described it as a mini vacation. You can probably find a class in relaxation techniques somewhere in your community. Try the Y or your local hospital or recreation department. Also bear in mind that some everyday activities can be very relaxing. Here are a few simple suggestions:

- Listening to your favorite music

- Reading a book

- Going for long walks

- Gardening

- Taking a long, hot bath

- Shopping (for some people)

Think about what relaxation strategies work best for you and list them here: ___

_____

_____

Reassure Yourself

Every once in a while, negative feelings such as guilt, grief, and selfishness rear their ugly heads. As the parent of an adult child with developmental disabilities, you may be particularly vulnerable to those feelings. You may berate yourself for not doing enough for your son or daughter, thinking that if only you spent more time with him or her, things would be so much better, and so forth. Remember that you are only a human being, not a saint.

When you're beset by these difficult feelings, you need to talk encouragingly to yourself and forgive yourself, just as you would forgive others for not being perfect. Remind yourself that you don't have all the time in the world, nor do you have all the patience in the world. You do the best you can most of the time. And sometimes you think only of yourself and your needs. But that's not only natural, it's fine.

For example, I used to take Susie to all the family gatherings, but now, as I'm getting older, I don't. When Susie is with me at a party, I feel like I have to watch her all the time, looking for signs of emotional overload. And then I have to convince her to leave before she has a complete meltdown. This makes me quite tense, and I can't really relax and enjoy myself. So now I've given myself permission to leave her at home occasionally without telling her where I'm going. Should I feel guilty? Am I really hurting Susie? Or is this the real world where we all have to make choices such as these?

What are some things your best friend would say to you when you start to feel guilty or selfish? List them here: _____

_____

_____

Life is full of ups and downs, and parents of adults with developmental disabilities know that better than most. We need to learn to take more pleasure during the good times and protect ourselves during the down times. When the going gets tough, you need to reassure yourself by reminding yourself of all the good times you and your child have experienced. Tell yourself that this difficult time will pass and the good times will return, as they always do. Then take an active role in making things better.

In reality, you are probably much more selfless than many people. If anything, you probably err on the side of devoting too much of yourself to your adult child with developmental disabilities. When the going gets tough, or if you're having a hard time doing things for yourself, remind yourself of everything you've given. You have nothing to be ashamed of and much to be proud of.

Reinforce Your Family Ties

Family ties provide a network of mutual support. If all of the members of your family are stressed by the care and worry of having an adult family member with developmental disabilities, you'll have a hard time supporting each other, much less having fun together. And families are supposed to have fun together, at least occasionally.

Sometimes this stress can be very hard on a marriage. As you begin to get used to the idea that it's okay to take time for yourself and take care of yourself, realize that you may also need to devote some time and attention to your marriage. Now is the time to begin rebuilding the love, understanding, and connectedness you once shared. You may need a therapist to help you reconnect.

If you feel that you've been shortchanging your other children, sit down and talk to them. Tell them how you feel and ask how they feel. You may find that they fully understand and support what you're doing to help their sibling with developmental disabilities. You can also arrange to spend some intensive one-on-one time with each of your other children.

Take some time to consider ways you can reconnect with your other family members. Also brainstorm on ideas for how you can have more fun together. If some of those ideas might help you renew or redefine yourself, or relax, all the better. Jot your ideas here:

_____

_____

_____

_____

Reward Yourself

Few people know how difficult your life sometimes is. Nobody rewards you for taking care of your adult child, although a rusty "I love you" from your son or daughter or a lopsided smile can do the job. You have to take pride in what you do, and you have to pat yourself on the back when you've accomplished something difficult, or even just when you've managed to persevere in your daily responsibilities. List five things you can pat yourself on the back for doing:

1. _____

2. _____

3. _____

4. _____

5. _____

Take a moment every day to remind yourself of what a good job you're doing. Also take pride in your child's accomplishments. These are like little gifts you get for loving and caring for him or her.

Feeling reassured that you're doing a good job is, in many ways, the best reward. But sometimes it's nice to reward yourself more tangibly. Here are a few suggestions for other ways you can reward yourself:

- Buy a gift for yourself, something you've always wanted.

- Go on an outing with friends.

- Take a long weekend getaway with your spouse or significant other.

- Get a massage or spa treatment.

List some ways you can reward yourself. Include relatively small rewards as well as big ones. _____

_____

_____

Now make a plan to do something special for yourself. Be specific: What will you do and when will you do it? _____

_____

_____

Next Steps

A key to enhancing your quality of life is to take good care of yourself. The eight Rs will keep you on track in this regard as you reassess your current situation and then start making small changes in your daily life. Learning to relax, nurture your relationships, reward yourself, and start following your dreams will all help you feel better about yourself and your life. Taking care of yourself will also give you more energy and clarity, which will help you come up with the best possible plan for your son or daughter.

As mentioned, there's a reciprocal quality to parent-child relationships, so another way of enhancing your quality of life is to enhance the quality of life of your adult child with developmental disabilities; what makes him or her feel good makes you feel good. It's a win-win situation, but it can be difficult because it might entail reevaluating some ways you and others view your child and interact with him or her. In the next chapter, we'll take a look at ways you can make your child's current situation better.

CHAPTER 4

Making Life Better for Your Son or Daughter

Although they feel safe and cared for, many adults with developmental disabilities report that they're bored and lonely (National Organization on Disability [NOD]/ Harris Survey 2000). This is because most of these adults have limited opportunities to socialize with their peers. Because they're usually unemployed or work very few hours, they can't use a work environment to find friends the way nondisabled adults do. They want to work, yet they often just sit at home watching television and slowly losing the skills they learned in school. One parent with a son with serious developmental disabilities living at home reported that her son's greatest disability was loneliness. Many adults with developmental disabilities who are living in the community also report being lonely and bored, especially if they live alone or with only one or two others. Their interests and strengths often remain untapped.

The purpose of this chapter is to help you make your son's or daughter's life as satisfactory as possible, regardless of where he or she lives. Some of the suggestions are relatively easy to follow; others require some soul-searching on your part. Finally, as you strive to enhance your adult child's life, you may have to train other caregivers to do the same.

All Dressed Up with No Place to Go

When our children were in school, their lives were filled with activities. They had classmates to interact with and enjoy. They had things to learn and do. But as soon as they graduated from school, most of these young adults found themselves with few places to go and little to do. No wonder many of them are bored or depressed.

When they were in school, they were away from their families quite a bit: five hours a day, five days a week, or even longer. As adults, they're often largely dependent on their families, not only for food and shelter, but for friendship and stimulation. So in essence, adults with developmental disabilities are often more dependent on family than when they were children. And unfortunately, this often causes parents to think of them as much younger than they are. Many professional caregivers still treat them as children, too.

"Perpetual Children"

People with developmental disabilities used to be viewed as perpetual children. Parents were told that they would reach a plateau and that their intelligence would never increase beyond that of a five-year-old. But that isn't true, is it? Of course our adult children continue to grow and change as they continue to learn and experience new things. Most of them understand more, say more, and do more. Lisa, a young woman with mild mental impairment, loves to add new words to her vocabulary. She says to her father, "I know, Dad, you're just being sarcastic," when he teases her. Right now she's trying out the word "paranoid," which she heard on TV.

Not only do these adults grow intellectually, they grow emotionally as well. Sometimes we forget that they have adult feelings, such as envy, competitiveness, hopefulness, pride, and pleasure in the company of a good friend. Many people are heedless of these feelings because they don't recognize them (and don't even believe they exist) in people with developmental disabilities. But you can see these feelings in a smile, a blush, a scowl, or an angry shake of the head. For example, Susie blushes when she mentions a certain young man she knows and ignores me when I ask if he's her boyfriend.

You must not allow yourself (or anyone else) to put off your son's or daughter's adulthood—for any reason. This is not to say you have to cut him or her loose from all parental protection. Health and safety issues still require you to be vigilant. But it's important for you to see your son or daughter as an adult, to treat him or her as an adult, and to encourage him or her to feel like an adult so that your child can lead a satisfying life—a life that is satisfying to *your child*.

What Does Being an Adult Mean?

Adulthood brings with it a sense of responsibility and a sense of freedom. Among other things, a responsible adult works in order to provide himself or herself and his or her family with food and housing; a responsible adult takes care of children and others in need of protection; and a responsible adult is a caring and generous friend.

The freedom that comes with being an adult is the freedom to make choices and to take control of one's life. Often called "self-determination," this includes choosing what clothes to wear and what to eat, going to bed when you please, choosing who to live with, and deciding where and how to live (bearing in mind any health and safety issues). Adulthood also brings with it certain privileges only adults have, like driving a car, voting, serving in the armed services, and getting married. Adult status also confers the dubious honor of being able to drink alcohol or buy cigarettes.

When it comes to your child with a developmental disability, adulthood may not necessarily entail a completely normal adult life, but a "normalized" life—as close as he or she can get to a normal life. This may mean that although your child may not drive a car, serve in the armed forces, or make enough money to buy his or her own home, and although your child may need support in many areas of life, he or she lives the life of an adult in terms of a sense of responsibility, freedom, and privilege.

It's important to note that an adult not only feels like an adult, he or she is seen as an adult by others. For example, you may need to ask yourself if your child really needs as much guidance as you offer. It's also important to encourage everyone who works with your child to not only care for and support him or her, but to treat him or her with the respect due to an adult.

How Do You "Build" an Adult?

But how do you give the adult with severe cerebral palsy the freedom to explore and make choices? How do you instill a sense of responsibility into an adult with moderate to severe intellectual disabilities? The first part of the answer is that you model these feelings and attributes for your son or daughter through the years (Greenbaum 1987). For example, if your adult child sees you or other adults caring for a young child, he or she will come to understand that this is what adults do.

My granddaughter Wendy used to spend several weeks a year at my house with Susie and me. When Wendy was about four (and Susie about twenty), I gave her a laminated list to use when we went shopping at the supermarket. I had actually gotten the list from the Arc in Grand Rapids and had originally bought a list for Susie, although Wendy didn't know that. One day when she was upstairs in Susie's room, Wendy cried, "There's my shopping list! I've been looking all over for it." Then she grabbed the list. Susie said, "My list," and tried to grab it back. Before I got upstairs they were both in tears.

My first reaction was to turn to Wendy and try to explain that the list was Susie's and that I would buy her another one. Wendy cried even harder. "No, it's my list," she sobbed. I turned to Susie with little hope and said, "Susie, Wendy is your niece. You're a grownup. She's just a little girl, and look how she's crying. Please let her have the list, and I promise that I will buy you another one." There was a long pause, and then

Susie said, "Aw right," and patted Wendy's head. Susie knew she was the grownup in this situation and she knew how grownups were supposed to act. Wendy, of course, acted like the child she was.

Modeling

If your son or daughter sees how you go about making choices or trying something new, he or she will begin to understand how adults do this. Consciously modeling these actions for your child as you go about your daily life is the key to helping him or her learn to be an adult. Modeling has been shown to be the preferred method of imparting information to a person with learning difficulties or developmental disabilities, rather than direct teaching (Deshler, Ellis, and Lenz 1996). Modeling is also a more respectful way of helping an adult with developmental disabilities learn something, rather than telling them what to do.

When your children were young, you modeled things for them all the time, and they imitated you. They walked like you. They imitated many of the phrases you used in talking to them or others. When Susie puts on her jeans, she nonchalantly leans against a wall with her hands in her pockets. I noticed one day that this is something I do. I guess Susie thinks it's cool.

You'll need to talk aloud as you model various actions; doing so helps your child understand your thought processes. You can say something like this: "Let me see. Should I wear a coat today? It's winter and it's going to be cold outside, so I'd better wear a coat." For trying a new food, you can say something along these lines: "What is that? I've never seen it before. John says it tastes good. I can try just a little bit to see if I like it." Other adults in your household can act as models, too.

Remember, you aren't teaching or telling; you're modeling, which means talking to yourself as you go about doing something so that your child can overhear you and observe you. Don't tell your child to "do it this way." Modeling communicates "this is the way I do something" without implying that your child must do it the same way.

Here's an example of how to model the everyday activity of using deodorant:

1. Let your daughter observe your routine after taking a shower.

2. Tell yourself (aloud) during that routine that you'd better be sure to use deodorant to keep yourself from smelling bad.

3. Let your daughter smell your deodorant to see how nice it smells.

4. You might suggest that your daughter smell her own armpits to see if they smell bad.

5. Ask your daughter if she would like to use some deodorant to keep smelling nice.

6. Shop with your daughter to buy her her own deodorant.

After modeling something a few times, you can encourage your child to try it out if he or she wants to. You may have to help out in the beginning. But eventually let your child proceed in his or her own way.

Encourage Participation in Activities of Daily Living

Let your child observe you as you go about the activities of daily living. Bring him or her with you into the kitchen when you cook and clean up. Encourage him or her to participate as much as he or she can. You can say, "Please bring me the salt and pepper," for example. You can model how to make a sandwich or prepare cereal for breakfast.

Lisa loves to make lunch for her family when she's home. She's gone from making sandwiches to making macaroni and cheese. She needed to learn how to operate the microwave, but the rest was easy. She had often observed others do it, so she felt she could.

Aaron, who has severe cerebral palsy and can neither talk nor care for his own daily needs, is always in the kitchen when his mother is preparing a meal. Using a head switch mounted on his electric wheelchair, he can activate many electrical appliances such as a mixer and food processor and can even pour from a cup using an electrified pourer designed by a family friend. The electric appliances are all adapted using a linkage tool to allow Aaron's head switch to control them.

Let your child observe you feeding the dog or cat, doing the laundry, and so on. And take him or her with you as you go shopping. When we shop, Susie gets the Cheerios, Raisin Bran, and Lactaid. Like many other nonreaders, she's good with brand names because their logos are usually so distinctive. Take your child when you go to the library or run other errands. If feasible, take him or her to work with you so that he or she can see what your work is about.

Lisa's father used to take Lisa to the polls when he voted. He often showed her what he was doing on the voting machine mock-up in front of the polling booth. One day she asked him if she could vote and said she thought she knew how. Now she votes in most elections—sometimes for the candidate her father opposes.

What daily living tasks does your son or daughter do now? _____

_____

_____

What tasks would your son or daughter like to learn? _____

_____

_____

Choose one of these tasks and describe how you would model it for your son or daughter. What steps would you take? _____

_____

_____

_____

After you've modeled a couple of activities, modeling others should come naturally. But you may want to write out or at least visualize how you'll model things the first few times you try this technique.

Health and Safety

Model good eating habits and talk about nutrition. Then back it up by buying less junk food. Substitute healthier foods your child likes to eat for at least some of the junk food he or she may be used to.

If your child is relatively mobile, don't park in handicap spaces at the store or movie theater; park further away and take the opportunity to walk. If you exercise, take your child with you. You can talk to a physical therapist or personal trainer about adapting exercises for your son's or daughter's particular needs.

Model the proper use of electrical appliances, such as the microwave and hair dryer. Susie doesn't use our gas stove. I think it's too dangerous and complicated for her. I may be wrong, but she does have difficulty turning her wrist to operate the knobs. Her direct care worker is helping her learn to use the washing machine, and she is quite enthusiastic about that.

What household appliance do you think your son or daughter would like to operate? _____

_____

_____

Write out the set of steps you'd use to model the safe operation of one of these appliances so that you can demonstrate its use to your son or daughter.

_____

_____

_____

_____

_____

Fire Drills

Don't forget fire drills. All licensed group living situations are required to have periodic fire drills, but no one requires parents to have home fire drills. Think of at least one escape route other than through the front door that your child can use to exit the house (with your help if necessary). You'll then need to model how he or she would leave the house in case of fire and then practice it every once in a while.

Write your evacuation plan here or on a separate piece of paper, and post it on a bulletin board or somewhere that other family members and caregivers can see it.

_____

_____

_____

_____

_____

Check with your local fire department to see if you can get a sticker to apply to the front of your house indicating that a person with disabilities lives in the house. This will help the firefighters be prepared to get your child out of the house in case of fire. And bear in mind that firefighters may wear some scary gear when fighting a fire. It would be helpful for your child to become familiar with how a firefighter in full regalia looks before a fire occurs so that he or she isn't afraid when a firefighter comes to help. Call your local fire station and explain the situation; then ask if you can bring your son or daughter to the station. It would be a good idea to do the same thing with the local police department so that your child will become familiar with their uniforms and see the police as friends, or at least as nonthreatening.

Provide the Trappings of Adulthood

Surround your adult child with the trappings of adulthood, based on his or her personal preferences. To begin with, this means making sure that he or she is dressed (comfortably) as an adult. Clothing should be in the current young-adult style, which may mean that it's a wee bit revealing or sexy to your way of thinking. (Lisa's grand-mother used to buy her "old lady" clothes. I used to buy Susie "little girl" clothes until one of my sons set me straight.)

If your child has special requirements in terms of clothing, try to make them as unobtrusive as possible. For example, Scott often drools due to his severe cerebral palsy and needs to wear a bib to mop up the spittle. His mother makes him bibs dyed to match his clothing so they're less noticeable.

For a daughter, see to it that she has access to makeup, nail polish, and perfume, and for a son, make sure he has access to the shaving cream and aftershave he prefers. Encourage your adult child with developmental disabilities to pay for these items with money earned at work or doing chores around the house. Give gifts appropriate to adult interests, for example, a CD or DVD player and CDs or DVDs. Other adult-type gifts include a basketball and hoop, supplies for art projects, a karaoke machine, a T-shirt with a favorite logo, or a gift certificate so that he or she can choose his or her own gift. However, this doesn't mean that you should never buy your adult child a stuffed animal if that's what she loves.

Give your child a section of the newspaper to look at, and offer him or her tea or coffee when you sit down to have some. Susie always asks for coffee, although she doesn't really drink it. Involve your adult child in adult activities. Take him or her with you to a baseball game, a meeting of an organization you belong to, or a jazz club. Lisa loves to go to the casino with her dad for an hour or two. She loves the slot machines with all their bells and whistles. He gives her ten dollars to start. If she wins, she keeps the money. If she loses, she stops and spends the rest of the time watching her dad play.

Encourage your adult child to socialize with other adults and help him or her get involved in adult activities. This can include working on a political campaign, volunteering in the community, or, like Mark, a young man with mild to moderate mental impairment, becoming a member of the Junior Chamber of Commerce. Or you might encourage your son or daughter to join a group of adults with disabilities in a social activity.

Many religious denominations and ethnic groups have rites and rituals through which members can pass when they reach adulthood, such as confirmations, bar and bat mitzvahs, and quinceañeras. Arranging for and adapting such rituals for your child can be a very meaningful way for him or her to understand and accept the mantle of adulthood.

Providing your son or daughter with the trappings of adulthood is a relatively easy thing to do. It may not be as profound as some of the other suggestions in this chapter, but it does set the stage.

List some trappings of adulthood that you can provide for your son or daughter.

_____

_____

_____

_____

Give Chores and Responsibility

Responsibility brings with it feelings of competence and self-worth, and it's one of the hallmarks of adulthood. You may wish that you yourself had less responsibility, but adults with developmental disabilities thrive on it—maybe because they rarely feel they can contribute much to the well-being of the family.

It's important to give your son or daughter chores and responsibilities he or she can handle successfully. Maria feeds the dog and takes him for a walk (and the dog also watches out for her). Susie sets the table and brings in the mail. She also pushes the shopping cart in the supermarket. CJ, who is a neat freak, straightens up the living room in his family home and puts everybody's junk away. His own room is neat as a pin. Lisa does the laundry when she's home.

Ask your child to do the last step in a complicated chore. For example, when making a bed, you can ask your child to pull the bedspread up over the pillows. You rarely have to ask an adult with a developmental disability for help more than once. And when you ask for help, watch his or her eyes light up. Responsibility is a gift for your child. It means that you respect and trust him or her, that you think he or she is competent. When your child helps out, don't forget to say thank you, and take every opportunity you can to recognize his or her contribution to the family.

List some things your son or daughter can already do to help you or others in the family, such as getting your slippers from your bedroom or bringing you a glass of water: _____

_____

_____

Think about whether your son or daughter can perform part of some chores now. What can he or she do? _____

_____

_____

What are some chores or responsibilities your son or daughter would like to have? _____

_____

_____

What kind of help or support would your son or daughter need to perform these chores? _____

_____

_____

_____

We tend to think in all-or-nothing terms when it comes to deciding whether an adult with developmental disabilities is able to do something or not. Remind yourself that your child can do parts of some tasks and you can do the other parts, or you can let him or her take the major responsibility for a task and offer your support as needed.

It's important for your child to know that he or she is able to help someone else, especially since others help him or her much of the time. Giving your son or daughter some responsibility, and a sense of interdependence, can help bring him or her into the adult world.

Don't Overprotect or Overcorrect

I'm going to go out on a limb and say that we all overprotect our adult children with developmental disabilities at least some of the time. It's very hard not to. They have needed our protection and support for so long that it's hard for us to let go. But we must, for their sake. Of course, health and safety is the bottom line, but we need to balance these factors against their need to grow up and make decisions for themselves.

For example, if your son has accompanied you to a particular store many times and he now wants to buy something by himself, let him go into the store and buy what he wants while you wait outside. (If it makes you too nervous, you can always peek inside—as long as he doesn't see you.) If your son is successful, think of how proud he will be to have purchased something himself. If he isn't successful, encourage him to try again and provide him with a little more support and practice next time.

What things would your son or daughter like to do independently? List them here: _____

_____

_____

_____

Consider whether your son or daughter can do at least some of these things, or a portion of certain things, independently, and describe what he or she can do:

_____

_____

_____

What are some ways you can encourage your son or daughter to do more things more independently? _____

_____

_____

_____

It's important to allow your adult child to try new things he or she wants to do, even if your child finds out he or she can't do them on his or her own. If your child isn't successful, or he or she is only partially successful, you can tell him or her that you'll help next time. Any success he or she does experience will give him or her the confidence to go on to try something else.

And sometimes not being successful can be a good learning experience, too. For example, Lisa had been pestering her father to teach her to drive, and her father kept putting off his answer. Finally, he had a good idea about how to handle it. Instead of just telling Lisa she couldn't drive, he took her out to a large, deserted parking lot one Sunday, and—after some instruction—let her try her hand at it. She drove the car haltingly while her dad helped her turn the wheel. After less than five minutes, she decided she had had enough. "It's really scary," she said. This approach showed Lisa that her dad respected her right to try driving, and it also taught her that driving isn't as appealing as she had thought—something she never would have learned if she hadn't gotten a chance to try it.

It's important to understand that adults with developmental disabilities need emotional and physical independence. How often does your son or daughter seem to be saying "Let me do it myself" when you do something for him or her? It may be easier or quicker, or you may be able to do it better, but your son's or daughter's sense of independence and self-worth is also at stake. Doing things for your child that he or she can handle on his or her own communicates disrespect and stifles his or her growth.

Allow your child to do those things that he or she can, in whatever way he or she can. If your child sets the table, restrain yourself from straightening out each place setting. If he or she helps fold the clothes and isn't very neat about it, tell yourself that he or she is doing the best he or she can and let it go at that. Limit any corrections to those necessary for health or safety. Other corrections are best done through your daily modeling of various activities and decision-making processes. (However, an occasional "Your slip is showing" or "Your fly is unzipped" is perfectly fine.)

Utilize Assistive Technology

Using assistive technology can help your child function more independently. Some common low-tech items are electric can openers, reachers (for items on higher shelves), electric toothbrushes, and Velcro shoe closures (no more "let me tie your shoes"). Telephones with programmed phone numbers and large finger pads can help your son or daughter call friends and family without your help. You can install a railing to help your child go up and down stairs or install grab bars in bathrooms. Some high-tech assistive technology can help people with severe physical disabilities turn lights on and off, turn the radio, TV, or other electronic devices on and off and adjust the volume, and so forth.

Sometimes all it takes is a little creativity to adapt knobs, handles, or switches so that your child can use them. Being able to use these things without asking for or waiting for help will give your child a feeling of competence and mastery. Go to your local hardware or home improvement store and check out the housewares, building supplies, and gadgets they sell. Many of the adapted utensils and appliances you need are already on the market.

What types of adaptations or assistive technology would enable your son or daughter to perform daily living tasks more independently? _____

_____

_____

Break the Cycle of Emotional Dependence

If your adult child won't let you out of his or her sight, if he or she insists that you and you alone help him or her, or if your child cries when you leave to go somewhere, your child is too emotionally dependent on you. But because this emotional dependence has built up over a long period of time, it may take time and patience to change the situation. Encouraging your child to do things for himself or herself as much as possible will help him or her feel less dependent on you. Move the process along by deliberately spending less time with your child and letting him or her do things without you hovering.

You have to learn to let go. Since it's likely that the day will come when you won't be able to take care of your child yourself, it's important to get your child used to others caring for him or her. Your child needs to get used to not having you around most of the time. Do this slowly but firmly, knowing that it's in his or her best interest to be less dependent on you in the long run. You can start by having a family member or friend take care of your child for a few hours, at first spending time with him or her at home. Once this is working well, they could go to a favorite restaurant together.

The next step would be for you to introduce your child to a professional caregiver by inviting the caregiver over to dinner and letting your child spend some time with him or her while you're in another room. The last step would be for you to leave your child at home with the professional caregiver for an hour or so and then gradually increase the length of time you're gone.

The good thing about this process of letting go is that it's gradual. You'll still be around to love your child as he or she becomes less emotionally dependent on you. Keep reminding yourself that your son or daughter is an adult and that most adults with developmental disabilities are able to separate themselves from their parents emotionally. Sure, your child may prefer to be with you, but he or she should be able to manage without you at times.

Staying Home Alone

One of the difficult things for adults with developmental disabilities is that they often must go where others are going and do what others are doing, whether they care to or not. This happens when caregivers feel that the person can't be left alone for reasons of safety. It's important to ask yourself whether your son or daughter really needs someone with him or her all the time or whether he or she can be safely left alone for an hour or two, or for an evening.

CJ, who comes and goes at will, sometimes prefers to stay home alone when the family goes out. He uses this time to clean up his room and arrange his things. Maria, who follows routines very well, is often left alone with the family dog when her parents go out. They always leave their phone number with her in case she has to call them for any reason. When Lisa asks to stay alone, her father feels comfortable leaving her at home for several hours at a stretch. However, she does need to be reminded not to answer the door or telephone, because she is very friendly and tends to tell complete strangers of her private affairs.

I don't leave Susie home alone for reasons of safety, but she's free to move about the house or go out in our front yard without me or anyone else hovering over her. She really doesn't like to have someone with her all the time. Where she lives, on the campus of a church-run facility, Susie is free to move about the campus on her own, and she's very happy about this.

Overprotection and overcorrection can smother your son's or daughter's feelings of competence and self-worth. Always question whether what you do for your child is necessary for his or her health or safety. If it isn't, tell yourself to back off. And don't feel alone; I often have to tell this to myself, too.

Communicate Respect

It's important to communicate respect as well as love. Respect makes people feel important and valued. Communicating respect means first appreciating and accepting who the person is and then demonstrating consideration for the person's feelings and preferences. We communicate respect when we let our sons and daughters do things for themselves. We communicate respect when we're willing to spend the time necessary to understand what they're trying to say to us and when we compliment or thank them. We communicate respect when we allow them to choose what they want to wear, who they want to spend time with, and what they want to eat.

It's important to respect their privacy, as well. Unfortunately, the level of support so many adults with developmental disabilities need limits their privacy. But even when helping them dress, for example, we need to allow them as much privacy as possible. This means knocking on your son's door and waiting for an okay before entering his room. Respect for privacy may also involve reminding your daughter (gently) that adults don't go out in public in their underwear or pajamas.

Don't Try to "Fix" Your Son or Daughter

As parents, we often want our children to look and act the way we think they should. We frequently feel this way even when they are adults. We forget that each is a unique individual with his or her own feelings, preferences, and values. Keep in mind that your child with developmental disabilities has probably accepted who he or she is. At a recent United Cerebral Palsy meeting, an adult with cerebral palsy said, "Don't keep trying to 'fix' me. I am not a toy." Everyone deserves respect, and, ultimately, that means accepting the person for all his or her abilities, disabilities, faults, and good points.

This doesn't mean that you can't keep striving to change and improve the situation surrounding your child. It does mean less or almost no correcting, criticizing, teaching, and saying no. It means that your son or daughter should largely be the one determining what he or she wants to do, how he or she wants to do it, when, and with whom.

Provide Opportunities to Make Choices

Self-determination is a cornerstone of a good life. The freedom to choose various aspects of one's life goes a long way toward having a satisfying life. Having someone else chose for you—where you should live, whom you should live with, or where you should work—can create a great deal of frustration, resentment, and unhappiness for the person who is given no say in the matter.

To prepare our sons and daughters for making major, life-altering decisions, we need to help them by modeling how we make choices. Begin by modeling simple, concrete, everyday choices, such as choosing what to wear or what to eat for breakfast. With time, start modeling more abstract things, such as choosing who to invite for dinner next week or what birthday present you should buy for a friend.

Most adults with developmental disabilities are fully capable of choosing their own friends, choosing their caregivers, and making decisions about where and how to live and work. Even if the person is nonverbal, most parents can tell who and what their son or daughter likes or dislikes by a smile or a gaze in a particular direction. Allowing your child to make choices has practical benefits, too. For example, he or she is likely to be much more cooperative with a caregiver he or she likes than one he or she dislikes.

Of course, health and safety must dictate the range of choices offered to adults with developmental disabilities. Susie often doesn't want to hold my arm when we cross the street, but I still insist on it because she still doesn't watch out for cars. However, when it comes to non-life-threatening issues, I do let her choose, and I abide by her choices (or try my best to). For example, because she doesn't know how to dress for the season, she might put on a sweatshirt and jacket when it's ninety degrees outside. If she can tolerate it, so can I (but I might point out that I'm wearing a short-sleeved T-shirt because it's so hot).

Ensuring that your child has many opportunities for making (and following through on) choices will help him or her fully participate in both minor and major decisions that affect his or her quality of life. Begin with concrete choices and move slowly to more abstract ones. At first, present only two alternatives. For example, ask your daughter whether she wants Raisin Bran or Cheerios for breakfast, or ask your son whether he wants to wear this T-shirt or that one, holding them up for him to see. The following list illustrates the range of choices you should give your child:

- What to watch on TV

- What movie to see

- What to buy

- What to eat

- When to go to sleep

- What to wear

- Who to invite for dinner

- Where to go

- Where to live

- Who to room with

- Where to work

- Who to hire as a caregiver

- Other: _____

- Other: _____

"Bad" Behavior Usually Means "No"

Susie is actually a very opinionated person (like most of the Greenbaums), but because of her limited speech we often don't know what she wants. But she certainly lets us know when she's displeased—by her behavior. She often yells or cries when she isn't allowed to do something she wants to do or feels she isn't being understood or doesn't want to do something someone else wants her to. She communicates her lack of choice through "bad" behavior, which usually means "No, I don't want to do that," "No, I don't like that," or "No, that's not fair."

Unfortunately, most people respond to this sort of bad behavior with punishment rather than trying to understand what the person is trying to communicate. This is a very demeaning and inappropriate way to interact with an adult. When adults with developmental disabilities exhibit bad behavior and tantrums, it is usually due to lack of choice or difficulty communicating what they want. Try to see such behavior as a means of communicating, and treat the situation as you would any disagreement between adults.

Try to figure out what your son or daughter wants to say or would like to do instead of just punishing him or her for "bad" behavior. Try to verbalize for him or her what you think he or she is trying to communicate. In this way you can set up a dialog of sorts. And then respect the choices that your child makes, even if you've tried to persuade him or her otherwise. Always take your child's feelings into account when doing something that involves him or her. It's too easy to disregard the feelings of people with developmental disabilities if it's expedient to do so.

One mother of a son with severe multiple disabilities reported that one day when she stopped by the group home where her son lived, he appeared rather upset. Glancing around, she happened to see another resident wearing her son's T-shirt—a shirt that had been given to him by his favorite uncle. When she questioned the caregiver as to why the other resident was wearing her son's T-shirt, she was told that this particular resident had run out of clean T-shirts, and besides, her son "wouldn't know the difference anyway." No wonder her son looked a little grumpy!

Nurture Interests, Abilities, and Talents

Interests, abilities, and talents are part of one's identity. You may focus so much on assisting your child and compensating for his or her disabilities that you have little time and energy to devote to encouraging his or her interests and talents. You might even be unaware of what those interests and abilities are. It's important to recognize and nurture these strengths; if you don't, they'll wither away.

It's very easy to underestimate Peggy. After all, she has quite a low IQ, uses a wheelchair, and has limited speech. But Peggy likes to write notes and cards to people. She can't really spell and prints her letter poorly, but if you ask her what she's just written, she'll read it to you and you'll be able to see that it makes sense. Unfortunately, her caregiver didn't understand this and thought Peggy was just scribbling at random. When Peggy would hand her a card she had made especially for her, the caregiver would laugh indulgently and put it away without asking Peggy what it meant. Soon Peggy stopped making cards for her. This is what happens when we don't recognize and encourage someone's ability.

Maria's talent is more obvious. She plays the recorder and knows many songs. She loves to play and is often asked to play at parties. She's very interested in music and her parents are now trying to find someone to give her piano lessons. Maria carries her recorder around wherever she goes and sometimes spontaneously bursts into song. Scott loves Broadway musicals. His parents have fostered that interest by taking him to New York City several times a year to see shows.

Often our kids inherit our interests and talents. Susie has quite an ear for music, something she gets from me. Actually, all my kids love music. Susie always asks me to turn on music when she's home. She distinguishes her taste in music from mine by saying "Mom's music" or "Susie's music." "Mom's music" is anything classical or ethnic. Susie's music is Elvis Presley, anything current with a strong beat, and "Oh Susannah" ("my song"). We often sing folk songs together.

As you develop your child's person-centered plan in the next chapter, you'll list his or her interests, abilities, and talents. This will help you ensure that your child has plenty of opportunities to pursue his or her interests and do things he or she is good at.

Locate Training and Support Services

Although you or another adult in your family can model most of the activities of daily living, you may feel that your child needs formal training in some areas, or you may feel that you aren't the best person to teach your child certain skills. Local community agencies and centers for independent living may be able to provide the needed training, and if not, they can probably refer you to someone who can.

These agencies often have workshops in independent-living skills for adults with various disabilities. They also generally have social workers on staff who can help with social skills, and contracts with psychologists and psychiatrists who can help solve behavior problems. In addition, these agencies can help determine what assistive technology your child might need and locate funding sources. Job coaches (discussed in chapter 7) can help with work-related skills and help your child access public transportation.

The person-centered plan you'll develop in the next chapter will help you assess the type and level of support your son or daughter needs in a variety of situations. This information will be useful as you begin to work with agencies to obtain the training, supports, and services he or she needs.

Locate Work Opportunities and Other Daytime Activities

One of the more important aspects of adult identity is work. This is true whether or not one has disabilities. As mentioned at the beginning of this chapter, most adults with developmental disabilities don't work, even though they want to. In chapter 7, you'll find suggestions for how to locate or develop work opportunities for your son or daughter. This isn't an easy task, but it's an important one. Beyond providing financial support, work also provides a feeling of self-worth and opportunities to socialize and as such is a key component of a satisfactory life for many people.

Provide Opportunities to Socialize with Other Adults

Adults with developmental disabilities rarely socialize with others outside their immediate family. This contributes to the sense of loneliness many of these people feel. When they were in school they saw their friends every day, but as adults, most of them rarely see their friends with or without disabilities. Their friends without disabilities tend to go their own way. And often there's no natural way to socialize with their friends with disabilities because so many of these adults don't work and don't participate in community activities. Plus, people with disabilities usually aren't fully integrated into society even though they may live in the community. Their neighbors may be kind to them or occasionally bake cookies for them, but adults with developmental disabilities usually aren't invited to socialize on a regular basis.

Community recreation and education programs, which serve the general public, often have cooking, sewing, woodworking, and other similar classes that might be both helpful and interesting for your child while also providing opportunities to socialize. See chapter 7 for a more in-depth discussion of different types of social activities your child might enjoy and how to find out which activities are available to him or her.

Help Them Survive Life's Challenges

Becoming an adult also means coping with life's challenges, the ultimate of which is the death of a parent. It is important that your son or daughter understand that death is not abandonment. It is equally important for your son or daughter to participate in the mourning process, even though some well-meaning caregiver or family member may want to "protect" your son or daughter or may feel that he or she cannot handle the grieving rituals. It is only by fully participating in the grieving process that your son or daughter will be able to deal with your death.

If possible, take your son or daughter to the funerals of close family or friends. Let your son or daughter participate in the rituals and see how people deal with grief. Model your own feelings and ways you try to cope with the death of someone you love. Explain what death means as best as you can. You can ask your pastor to help you.

As hard as it is for you, tell your son or daughter that some day you will die. Explain that there will always be people around to love and take care of him or her— and tell your child who these will be: close family members, professional caregivers, or circle of friends (see chapter 5).

It may take your child a long time to understand all of this, so you may have to remind him or her of these things from time to time.

I know this will make you sad, but if you prepare your son or daughter as best as you can, he or she will be able to cope with the grief and loss of a parent.

Modifying the Current Situation

After reading this chapter, you may want to work on one or two areas to help your son or daughter take on a more adult role and enhance his or her current situation. You may need to rethink how you (and others) have been relating to your child, and you may need to question whether there are better ways to do some things that are more in his or her best interests than the habits both of you have probably gotten into. It's likely that you'll also need to educate other members of the family and professional caregivers about how to help your son or daughter become more adult and lead a more satisfactory life.

IDENTIFYING A FEW AREAS FOR CHANGE

Wholesale changes can be threatening for any of us and difficult to accomplish, even when they're for the best. As you work to help your son or daughter take on a more adult role, it's probably best to focus on just a few areas at a time. Use the assessment below to help you decide what sorts of changes would be most beneficial.

Describe ways you treat your son or daughter as an adult: _____

_____

_____

Describe how you encourage participation in activities of daily living: _____

_____

_____

What trappings of adulthood does your son or daughter currently have? _____

_____

_____

Describe your son's or daughter's chores and responsibilities: _____

_____

_____

Describe how you communicate respect: _____

_____

_____

Describe how you take your son's or daughter's feelings into account: _____

_____

_____

Describe how you provide opportunities for your son or daughter to make choices:

_____

_____

Describe how you nurture his or her interests and talents: _____

_____

_____

Does your son or daughter work or participate in community activities? Yes No

If yes, please describe: _____

_____

_____

Describe your son's or daughter's opportunities to socialize: _____

_____

_____

Are there some areas you could improve upon? Choose two areas in the above list and describe how you can make changes or modifications in your son's or daughter's life to enable him or her to function like an adult. Adapt the suggestions in this chapter to your son's or daughter's interests, needs, and abilities, and check in to find out what he or she would like to do. Remember, you're providing opportunities and modeling new activities and behaviors, not teaching them.

1. _____

   _____

2. _____

   _____

Going shopping together for the trappings of adulthood can be a lot of fun. Working together in the kitchen, or even just observing, is something most people like to do. Tailoring household responsibilities to the capabilities of your son or daughter may take some creativity on your part. But once you figure this out, you'll see how happy your son or daughter will be to help.

If you find that an activity you've chosen is becoming aversive, change the activity or drop it. The goal is to enhance your son's or daughter's life by finding adult activities he or she enjoys participating in. After you've accomplished two changes, you can pick two more to work on.

Next Steps

Now that you've begun to work on enhancing your child's current situation, you can begin to look to the future. Chapter 5 discusses how planning for the future will be beneficial for both you and your child, and as you'll see, there are some benefits inherent in the planning process itself. The person-centered approach we'll take focuses on your child's interests, preferences, and support needs.

CHAPTER 5

Beginning the Planning Process

I recently asked several groups of parents about their goals for their adult children with developmental disabilities, and their answers seemed to reflect the goals parents have for all their children: "I want him to be safe and happy and to live in a caring environment." "I want her to be productive and have opportunities to learn new things—things she wants to learn, not things professionals want her to learn." "I want people to respect him as a person with thoughts and feelings." Getting more specific, many parents added such things as "I don't want her sitting around all day watching television" or "I hope he gets a chance to go bowling once a week. He really loves it."

Most parents also said something along the lines of "I want to make sure that there's someone to look out for him" or "I want her to have a caregiver who is a good person." Attaining these goals isn't merely the luck of the draw. You can't just sit back and hope good things will happen. These goals can only be achieved through active planning on the part of parents and family. Yet fewer than half of the parents of adults with developmental disabilities make a plan for the future of their son or daughter (DeBrine et al. 2003).

When planning for the future, one of the most important principles is to base any plans on your child's preferences. All too often, parents of adults with developmental disabilities make plans based on what they think is good for their sons and daughters without asking them what they want. In this chapter, you'll focus on who your child is—his or her personality, interests, strengths, preferences, and needs. Compiling this information is the starting point of any planning process for your child.

The Importance of Planning

The importance of planning can't be overstated. When parents of adults with developmental disabilities die or become unable to care for them, these adults often have to move to an unfamiliar place with unfamiliar people in addition to dealing with the terrible shock of their parent dying or becoming less available to them (Dowling and Hollins 2003). This can be very traumatic. An emergency placement is usually not the best place for a person to live, and there are often long waiting lists for more desirable spots.

Planning can cover these types of emergencies. You can make arrangements for your child in the event that you become seriously ill or die. It's even preferable for your child to make the transition while you're still in good health. If your child has already moved out of your family home and has become adjusted to a home in the community, he or she won't have to deal with displacement as well as grief.

Benefits of Planning

Planning isn't easy. It's time-consuming and challenging. But the rewards for your child—and for you—make it worth every minute you spend on the process. It will allow both you and your child to have a strong say in what happens to him or her when you're gone and ensure that he or she has a good place to live, someone to take care of him or her, and all of the supports he or she needs to live a good life. Systematic planning will help you and your family organize your thoughts, weigh different options, and work step-by-step toward your goal.

Planning allows you to prepare your child for the inevitable changes that life brings. You too will reap some benefits. Having a plan for your child's future can alleviate much of your stress and worry and bring hope to your life.

Why Parents Don't Make Plans for the Future

Many people simply don't plan for the future. They don't want to think about their own mortality. They don't even make out a will, much less arrange for guardianship of any young children. And parents of adults with developmental disabilities are no exception.

There are many other reasons parents of adults with developmental disabilities don't plan for their son or daughter to move out of the family home into a situation that is unknown. Many of these parents don't know what the possibilities are. They can't conceive of their children living on their own—and many of them can't live on their own. They don't know about the services and supports available to help their son or daughter live away from the family home. Even if they are aware of some of the options, they worry about how their son or daughter will feel living with strangers and whether caregivers will be kind and thoughtful and do what needs to be done.

Some of these parents don't trust the service delivery system or professionals. Perhaps an agency or professional recommended institutionalization for their son or daughter many years ago. Or perhaps they've had unsatisfactory or upsetting interactions with agencies in the past. They might have felt that no one listened to them or respected their opinions. Promises might have been made and then not kept. These parents might find it hard to believe that things have changed.

Many parents spend so much time and energy providing their adult children with the necessities of daily living that they feel they don't have time to plan. Or they may have begun to plan, perhaps even several times, but then felt overwhelmed at how large and complex a task it was. And often, parents of adults with developmental disabilities become so anxious and depressed when they think about the future that they simply refuse to think about it.

This chapter will address all of these reasons for not planning. The rest of the book will outline the various living situations available, offer guidance on how to find good caregivers, and help you clarify what supports are available and how to obtain them. It will help you negotiate the world of community agencies and some of the bureaucracies you may have to deal with. And, most importantly, it will help you develop a plan that suits the particular needs and preferences of your adult child with developmental disabilities.

Confront Your Worst Fears for the Future

When you think about your child's future without you, you might imagine the worst and then get weighed down by worry and despair. Putting your worst fears down on paper will help you confront them and begin to figure out how to deal with them.

What are your nightmares when you think about your son's or daughter's future? _____

_____

_____

_____

_____

What is the worst thing that could happen? _____

_____

Now think of this nightmare not as an inevitability, but as a problem to be solved. First of all, you'll need information about the supports and services that community agencies provide for adults with developmental disabilities. You'll need information about various residential and work options and how to locate well-trained professional caregivers who will be committed to helping your son or daughter. Chapters 6 through 9 will discuss all of these issues and give you guidance on how to obtain more in-depth information about the various options available. Then, armed with this information, you can start planning for the future systematically—and creating a plan that will prevent your nightmare from becoming reality.

Sometimes there are sources of support that you didn't know you could count on to help you through a nightmare situation. I recently confronted one of my worst nightmares: Susie, an adult, out of control in public, screaming, yelling, and inconsolable. While we were flying back home from California, Susie told me she had to go to the bathroom. She used the bathroom without incident, but just as she was stepping out of the bathroom, the plane hit some turbulence and Susie was thrown off balance. I caught her before she fell, but she started to scream and the plane continued to bump. Two flight attendants rushed to our side and asked me what the problem was. I explained over Susie's screams that she was afraid of falling and asked if she could sit down for a moment. Two strangers sitting nearby immediately jumped up and gave us their seats. As soon as Susie was comfortably seated she started to relax, soothed by the woman (another stranger) next to her, who slowly and calmly asked her what her name was and then introduced herself and continued talking to her. After a few minutes, I told Susie that we'd have to go back to our seats soon and asked her to tell me when she was ready. And a minute or two after that, Susie quietly said, much to my surprise, "I ready." I warned Susie that the plane would continue to bump, but said that I would hold her tight and wouldn't let her fall. As we haltingly made our way back to our seats, no one stared at us; they just went about their business.

I learned several things from this situation. First of all, strangers can provide help I never counted on. They can be amazingly kind and intuitive even if they've never met a person like Susie. Second, Susie, summoning resources I never knew she had, was able to help herself by understanding the situation and controlling her anxiety. Lastly, but perhaps most importantly, I learned that Susie and I could survive one of our worst nightmares.

Hopes and Dreams for the Future

Now let's turn to the opposite side of the coin. Think about the ideal future for your son or daughter—a future that fits his or her needs, abilities, and preferences. Visualize it and describe it in detail, including living arrangements, activities, and who he or she is with:

_____

_____

_____

_____

_____

_____

Keep this dream in mind as you read the next few chapters and think about various living and work situations, activities, and professional caregivers. Measure your dream against each option.

Raise Your Expectations

Sometimes parents of adults with developmental disabilities have aspirations for their children that are too low, just as society has. We can't imagine how they can survive living away from us or how they can hold a job. Yet today's adults with developmental disabilities have accomplished much more than we ever dreamed of:

- They have gone to school with nondisabled children.

- Most of them have learned to read—at least to some extent.

- They have participated in sports and cheered for their favorite teams.

- Some of them have gone on to higher education.

- They have found friends.

- Some of them have jobs, and many are volunteering in the community.

- Some of them have married and have children of their own.

People often perform as others expect them to. If you have low expectations of your child, he or she will be more likely to perform at a low level. If you have high expectations (within reason), he or she will probably rise to the occasion. As you dream about the future and begin to plan, it's time to set your sights higher.

Setting Goals

Goals drive any planning process. They help us stay focused on where we want to go and keep us energized and motivated as we work to attain them. It's likely that you already have a general long-term goal for your child, along the lines of locating a safe, caring, and stable environment. This is a good start, but ultimately your goals should be as specific as possible to help you achieve the outcome you want.

By the time you've finished working through this book, you should be able to revise this relatively general goal to specify the type of living situation you have in mind and the specific support services your son or daughter will need. You may find that you want to specify the location of the residential situation, such as within an hour's drive of a certain sibling. You'll also be able to include details about work and other meaningful activities and ideal caregivers. Then, together with your child, you'll decide when you want to attain these goals. That might be within one or two years, in about five years, or even longer.

Goals need to be realistic if they are to be attainable. On the other hand, be sure not to sell your son or daughter short because you think the "powers that be" won't go along with your wishes. Community agencies are much more responsive to individual needs and preferences than they used to be.

You need to set both long-term and short-term goals. Short-term goals can be steps along your path to long-term goals, or they can be independent goals. In either case, short-term goals should be things you can achieve easily and in a short time frame. This will allow you to see progress more quickly, helping you feel more hopeful and motivated to achieve your long-term goals. If you haven't already set some goals for improving your own quality of life, look back to chapter 3 and identify some reasonable short-term goals for yourself. Do the same for your son or daughter, using the ideas you came up with at the end of chapter 4.

Your long-term goal for your child is a larger and more complex prospect. Simplify the process by breaking it down into specific subgoals. Arranging for a good life for your child will involve the following subgoals:

- Locating a residential situation that you think is appropriate for your child (covered in chapter 6)

- Arranging work and other meaningful activities for your child (covered in chapter 7)

- Locating well-trained and dedicated professional caregivers (covered in chapter 8)

- Accessing community agencies that provide services and funding (covered in chapter 9)

These subgoals can, in turn, be subdivided still further as needed.

Planning Checklist

Use the following planning checklist to keep you on track for attaining your subgoals. Everything on the checklist will be covered in upcoming chapters. Because it will take some time to work through the entire list, you might want to mark this page or make a photocopy of the checklist, so you can easily refer to it at any point in time. Although you'll probably research and plan separately for each subgoal at first, each part of the plan impacts the others. For example, when you plan for your child's residential situation, you will want to take into account the caregivers and amount of support available at the residence.

1. Understand your son's or daughter's preferences, interests, and needs as described in each area below.

2. Decide on the type and level of support services your son or daughter needs for daily tasks.

3. Locate information regarding various options available in the community of your choice (residential situations, work opportunities, activities, and so on).

4. Visit and observe various options, if feasible. Take your son or daughter with you.

5. Discuss the options with your son or daughter and with other members of your family.

6. Visualize your son or daughter in each setting. What types of supports will he or she need in each setting? How will he or she feel in each setting?

7. Use a chart of pros and cons to evaluate each setting and discuss the pros and cons with your son or daughter and other family members.

8. Make a decision, then identify a second choice and even a third choice.

9. Develop your own options if none of the existing ones are acceptable to you.

You'll probably identify other specifics you need to work out as you proceed in the planning process. For example, if your child will move to another state to be near a sibling, your child will need to be evaluated by the new state to determine his or her eligibility to receive services and supports from that state. You'll need to find out how he or she can become a resident of that state in order to access financial benefits that state offers. In any case, your plans will have to be individualized and personalized, taking into account your child's preferences, your opinions and resources, and the agencies who will be providing funding.

Person-Centered Planning

Whatever plans you make should be based on your child's interests, preferences, needs, and strengths. This is the heart of person-centered planning and the focus of the rest of this chapter. Person-centered planning ensures that your plan will be tailor-made to fit your son or daughter. Of course, your own values and your concerns for your child are important as well.

Person-centered planning is a process in which the person with a developmental disability, along with his chosen friends and family, arrive at a plan based on his or her preferences, health and safety needs, and the support services he or she needs in order to attain his or her life goals. Community agency staff should also be a part of the planning process in order to consider support needs and funding issues. However, person-centered planning means that the focus is on the person, not on a set of services offered to all by the community agency.

Helping plan a good life for your child means that you and the others involved in the process first need to get to know your son or daughter as a unique individual. For that reason, you'll begin by gathering as much information as possible about your child: his or her personality, likes and dislikes, friends, preferred activities, and how he or she communicates, as well as the supports he or she needs for the activities of daily living.

Your Son or Daughter Is a Unique Individual

Because we've lived with our children for such a long time, we may have become so accustomed to them that we barely see them for who they are. They are usually fixed in our minds in a particular way, and that's that. This can be as true of husbands and wives as it is of parents and children. We often miss the subtle changes, and even the not-so-subtle changes, that are a part of everyone's lives and that make life so interesting.

A while back, a neuropsychologist at our local hospital asked me to keep track of Susie's vocabulary. In monitoring this, I discovered that she had added hundreds of words to her receptive vocabulary and was now speaking largely in complete, though short, sentences! If the neuropsychologist hadn't asked me to keep track, I wouldn't have noticed.

Some parents of adults with severe or multiple developmental disabilities may think they have no idea what their son or daughter feels or thinks. When pressed, however, these parents realize there's a certain smile for something their son or daughter likes, or a lack of cooperation with a caregiver he or she doesn't like. We need to believe in the fundamental capability of our adult children with developmental disabilities. With this in mind, take some time to really look at your son or daughter and describe the unique person he or she is. Also ask your other family members and children, your friends, and any long-term caregivers for their observations.

It can be difficult for me to figure out what my daughter Susie wants. Often my only clues are a certain light in her eyes or a sudden alertness. At those times, I try to read her mind. Through the years, my other children have often pointed out things Susie wants. For some reason, they seem to be better at this than I am. For example, when Susie was still in elementary school, my daughter Sara told me that Susie wanted me to buy her some overalls. Up to that point I had been dressing her in dresses. Sara said that all the kids were wearing overalls and that Susie wanted to wear them, too. So I asked Susie if she wanted to wear overalls, and she vigorously nodded her head yes, with a big smile. When I asked her if she wanted to wear dresses, she shook her head no. I was clearly out of touch.

Be sure to try to get input directly from your son or daughter. What would he or she say about himself or herself? Seth, who has relatively severe cerebral palsy, described himself, speaking very slowly and laboriously, as follows: "Seth is a tall, handsome fellow when he isn't sitting in his wheelchair. He has blue eyes and brown hair. He tends to drool a bit when he talks too much, but then, who's perfect?" On the other hand, my daughter Susie can't describe herself at all (except when she gets all dressed up and twirls around saying "cute!"), but she can usually answer yes or no when it comes to her likes and dislikes.

Also seek input from those who know your child best. When we were ready to develop Susie's person-centered plan, I invited her sitter Penny (who Susie loves), her brother Josh (who flew in from California for the occasion), Sister Margaret Mary (her house mother from Our Lady of Providence Center), and a longtime family friend to help describe Susie and develop her plan. You can invite others who know your child and want to help.

Why It's Important to Describe Your Son or Daughter

The purpose of writing out a description of your child is to ensure that service providers who work with your him or her really know who your child is. This allows them to design individualized and appropriate supports.

Too often the supports provided depend on what's available at the time rather than the person's needs and wants. People are made to fit the rules and regulations of a group living situation or work setting, especially when individual preferences aren't known. A written description of your child's likes and dislikes can be given to a supervisor or service provider to ensure that child is provided with the supports he or she needs to live life in the way he or she prefers.

Use the following lists to help you describe your child and identify his or her likes and dislikes. Some of the lists may overlap, and some may be missing descriptive words you want. Add whatever is needed to really capture your child's personality, strengths, interests, and needs. If your child has difficulty communicating, it will probably be more difficult to fill out the checklists. But don't let yourself get away with just checking a few things. You probably know much more about your child than you think you do.

The following checklists address many of the important components of a good person-centered plan. Be sure to check everything that applies, and add to the checklists whenever necessary. Everyone grows and changes over time, including people with developmental disabilities. You should revisit your child's person-centered plan every six months or so to be sure that the plan reflects his or her growth and current needs, interests, and abilities. So rather than filling in the form below, you might want to make a photocopy (or several), so you'll always have a fresh copy to work with.

PERSON-CENTERED PLAN

Date: _____

Full name: _____

Likes to be called: _____

Address: _____

_____

Phone number: _____

Strengths

What are your son's or daughter's strong points? What are the things he or she does relatively well? Check off all that apply and add anything not listed.

_____ Setting the table

_____ Doing arts and crafts

_____ Making the bed

_____ Cooking

_____ Working or employment

_____ Remembering people's names

_____ Looking nice

_____ Helping others

_____ Playing a musical instrument

_____ Taking care of pets

_____ Paying for things at the store

_____ Playing a sport

_____ Other: _____

_____ Other: _____

_____ Other: _____

Interests and Preferred Activities

What are some things your son or daughter would like to do? What are his or her interests?

_____ Visiting family

_____ Having friends over

_____ Going on vacation

_____ Participating in Special Olympics

_____ Going to concerts, the circus, plays, and other shows

_____ Interacting with pets or other animals

_____ Interacting with babies or small children

_____ Doing arts and crafts

_____ Keeping busy

_____ Watching TV

_____ Writing letters

_____ Listening to music

_____ Looking at photographs of family and friends

_____ Dancing

_____ Going to movies

_____ Bowling

_____ Swimming

_____ Playing basketball

_____ Sewing, crocheting, or knitting

_____ Grocery shopping

_____ Working

_____ Having books read to him or her

_____ Doing physical activities

_____ Playing electronic games

_____ Playing games on the Internet

_____ Eating out

_____ Attending sports events

_____ Going for a walk

_____ Other: _____

_____ Other: _____

_____ Other: _____

Dislikes

What does your son or daughter dislike? What are some things he or she refuses to do? What are some things that upset him or her? You may want to provide more details or explanations of why on a separate sheet of paper, which you should keep with this plan.

_____ Loud noises

_____ Snow and ice

_____ Certain foods (list them: _____)

_____ Changes in routine

_____ Certain types of TV shows (list them: _____)

_____ Being told what to do

_____ Certain people (list them and explain why: _____)

_____ Having nothing to do

_____ Someone touching his or her things

_____ Large gatherings of people

_____ Other: _____

_____ Other: _____

_____ Other: _____

Personality Traits

How would you describe your son's or daughter's personality? One's personality is generally made up of good points and bad points. Most of us have the following traits to some degree. Place an "O" next to a trait your son or daughter often displays, an "S" next to a trait he or she sometimes displays, and an "R" next to a trait he or she rarely displays. Add any other traits that are descriptive of your son or daughter.

_____ Wants to be helpful

_____ Outgoing, sociable

_____ Sensitive to other people's feelings

_____ Good sense of humor

_____ Generally happy

_____ Anxious

_____ Easily frightened

_____ Easily upset

_____ Often needs reassurance or encouragement

_____ Independent

_____ Eager

_____ Curious

_____ Sad

_____ Easily frustrated

_____ Competitive

_____ A leader

_____ Has temper outbursts

_____ Shy or quiet

_____ Opinionated

_____ Easily led

_____ Bossy

_____ Other: _____

_____ Other: _____

_____ Other: _____

Communication Style

How does your son or daughter communicate? This can be a difficult question if your child is nonverbal. But if you think about it, there are many ways your son or daughter communicates. Check all that apply:

_____ Gestures, pointing

_____ Facial expressions

_____ Pulling at people

_____ Pushing things away

_____ Throwing things he or she doesn't want or like in the trash

_____ Sign language

_____ Specific sounds indicating words

_____ Eye movements

_____ Limited speech (short phrases, single words)

_____ Speech that can be understood by others

_____ Augmentative communication device (describe: _____)

_____ Can accurately describe his or her feelings

_____ Can accurately describe cause and effect

_____ Can communicate needs and wants

_____ Can follow one- or two-step directions

_____ Can follow three-step directions

_____ Other: _____

_____ Other: _____

_____ Other: _____

How does your son or daughter communicate happiness or agreement? _____

_____

_____

How does your son or daughter communicate unhappiness, anger, frustration, or
not wanting to do something? _____

_____

_____

Problematic or Challenging Behavior

Frustration, anger, and unhappiness can lead to problematic behavior as your son or
daughter strives to communicate feelings, preferences, and needs. This behavior can
include hitting, tantrums, self-injurious behavior, and so on.

Does your son or daughter have any behavioral issues? _____

Please describe problematic behaviors: _____

_____

_____

When do these occur? _____

_____

_____

What is usually the cause? _____

_____

_____

When your son or daughter is upset (for whatever reason), what are the best ways
to calm him or her? _____

_____

_____

Circle of Friends

Think about the people your son or daughter loves and who he or she would choose to be friends with. This can include family, friends, caregivers, job coaches, social workers, Sunday school teachers, and so on. These are the people your son or daughter likes to be with, likes to call on the telephone, or likes to invite over. They are also the people your son or daughter might to turn to for support or comfort.

In the center of the circle below, write your son's or daughter's name. In the other two circles, write the names of the people your son or daughter loves or cares for. In the middle circle write his or her closest friends. In the outer circle, write his or her more distant friends. To the outer circle, you can add other people who love and support your son or daughter. This is your son's or daughter's circle of friends.

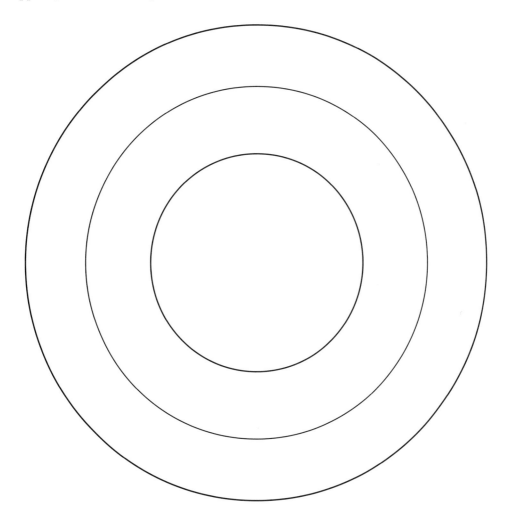

This circle of friends can form a support group for your son or daughter as he or she moves from your home out into the community or be of help in other difficult situations.

What Supports Does Your Son or Daughter Need?

In the following list, check off the activities your son or daughter needs help with. Using the numbers "0," "1," "2," and "3," describe the type of support you and others are currently providing for your son or daughter. Use "0" for items where no assistance is required, "1" to designate verbal prompting, "2" for some hands-on assistance, and "3" for complete physical assistance. For a more complete description of the types and intensity of support your son or daughter needs, you can use the Supports Intensity Scale of the American Association on Intellectual and Developmental Disabilities (see Resources).

Personal Care

_____ Getting out of bed

_____ Getting dressed

_____ Brushing teeth

_____ Toileting

_____ Shaving

_____ Washing face and hands

_____ Bathing

_____ Eating

_____ Selecting clothing appropriate to the weather

_____ Managing menstrual period

_____ Getting ready for bed at night

_____ Other: _____

_____ Other: _____

_____ Other: _____

Health and Safety

_____ Taking medications

_____ Crossing the street

_____ Fire and water safety

_____ What to do in case of an emergency

_____ Choosing healthful foods

_____ Avoidance of dangerous situations

_____ Protection against predatory or exploitative people

_____ Other: _____

_____ Other: _____

Daily Living Tasks

_____ Cleaning

_____ Operating appliances

_____ Managing money

_____ Shopping

_____ Preparing meals

_____ Cleaning up after meals

_____ Other: _____

_____ Other: _____

_____ Other: _____

Mental Health

_____ Communicating needs

_____ Making appropriate decisions

_____ Managing anger

_____ Managing anxiety

_____ Other: _____

_____ Other: _____

_____ Other: _____

Other Uses for Person-Centered Plans

Person-centered planning has many uses beyond forming the basis of a long-term life plan for a person with developmental disabilities. Community agencies often use person-centered planning to develop their individualized service plans for the following year. In that process, you, your child, and whomever you invite (friends, other family members, or professionals who know your child well) will sit down with agency staff and develop an individualized support system for your son or daughter.

Direct care workers can use person-centered plans to plan daily activities. This will help them ensure that your child's daily activities are individualized and appropriate for him or her. After considering the information you've gathered, direct care workers will provide the type and amount of support your child needs in order to do the things he or she wants to do.

You and other family members can use person-centered planning at home in the same way. It's important for everyone involved in your child's life to become as aware of his or her interests and strengths as they are of his or her needs for support. Your child's interests are the things that bring him or her pleasure, fulfillment, and a sense of productivity (as is true for all of us). Supports are simply the means of helping him or her achieve his or her goals.

Next Steps

The person-centered planning process is the beginning point in planning for your child's future. Chapters 6 through 9 will provide you with basic information about living arrangements, employment options and other fulfilling activities, finding a good caregiver, and community agencies. All of this information will help you develop specific goals appropriate to your child. Chapter 10 will help you bring everything together into a detailed plan. It will also offer guidance on how you can ensure that the plan is followed even after you're gone.

Remember, your child needs to be involved in the process, too. As much as possible, you need to include your child in all decisions affecting your child and his or her future. You may need to translate the information you learn into terms your child can understand. Taking your child along when you visit some of potential residences, workplaces, and caregivers is an even better way to help him or her understand what's going on and help him or her make informed decisions. Working together, you and your child can decide on a tentative goal in a particular area and then determine the amount and types of support needed to reach each goal.

CHAPTER 6

Finding a Good Place to Live

It's estimated that 76 percent of adults with developmental disabilities live at home with their parents (Fujiura and Park 2003). Most parents feel that this is the safest and most caring option for their adult son or daughter. And it probably is. After so many years, we know the things our sons and daughters like—or dislike. We can anticipate their needs. And we accept them for who they are and can provide them with unconditional love (most of the time).

But there are also major drawbacks to this arrangement, both for parents and for the adult with developmental disabilities. For parents, the drawbacks involve the stress of physically caring for their son or daughter, limitations on their work and career opportunities, and restrictions on their social lives. And though you may find it surprising, the drawbacks can be even greater for the adult with developmental disabilities. For them, negatives include isolation from their peers, limited opportunities to participate in activities typical of young adults, continued emotional dependence on their parents, and a lack of challenge that can stifle growth.

Parents with adult children with disabilities living at home are caring parents. If you're in this situation, you probably feel you understand your child's needs better than anyone else possibly can. I've been there and I understand these feelings. I too believe that no one will love or understand my daughter as well as I do (except, perhaps, my other children). But through the years, I've found that wherever she is, there is always at least one professional caregiver who does understand her and love her and another who challenges her to be the best she can be. And I've come to realize how much Susie enjoys the community in which she lives. As a weekend at home with me comes to a close, she eagerly asks, "What time leave see my buds?"

Deciding where your child should live can be a daunting task, but you don't have to start from scratch. This chapter will provide you and your child with information about different types of living arrangements to help you understand your options.

Deciding Whether Your Home Is the Best Place

It's true that you can provide a kind of love, affection, and acceptance that your child may have difficulty finding in the outside world. But sometimes love isn't enough. If there are several children and adults living in your home and lots of activity, this probably provides enough stimulation and opportunities to socialize that your adult child will continue to benefit from living at home. But if all your other children are gone and only one or two elderly parents remain at home, your child's world might be too narrow, and he or she might be better off living outside the family home in a situation that provides more stimulation.

Even so, if you can provide social opportunities and help maintain your child's friendships outside the family home, and if your child is involved in community activities, then he or she will probably continue to benefit from living in your home. If, however, your child doesn't have most of these opportunities, or if you're wearing down and feeling quite stressed, then it's time for you to consider finding another place for your child to live.

One-quarter of all parents caring for an adult son or daughter with developmental disabilities are over sixty years old (Fujiura and Park 2003). These parents must find a satisfactory living situation for their adult child outside the family home, and they need to do so right away. They are not going to live forever. Helping your child move out of your home while you're still around or still able to help him or her adjust may be the best thing you can do for your child at this stage of your life.

Moving In with a Brother or Sister

Some parents think it would be nice for their son or daughter to move in with a brother or sister. And many families do just that. The pros and cons of this arrangement are similar to those of having your child live at home with you. On the other hand, many parents don't want their other children to become worn down by caregiving, as they have been. How your other children feel about this option is the most important criteria, so be sure to discuss it with them first. If it seems to be a viable option, involve all of your family members in the decision-making process, including your adult son or daughter with developmental disabilities.

Benefits to Moving Out

Current research tells us that there are many benefits to the entire family when an adult with developmental disabilities moves out of the family home (Seltzer, Krauss, and Magana 1998). Benefits to the other children in the family include an improved relationship with their brother or sister with developmental disabilities and less worry about what the future holds for their brother or sister (Seltzer et al. 2005). Benefits for parents include less stress, more time and energy for their other children (and grandchildren), and less worry about the future of the son or daughter with developmental disabilities. It's reassuring to see that your son or daughter can survive and grow in a different living situation, without your continued presence. And once you see how much your child enjoys his or her new home, you may be able to take a much-needed vacation (perhaps your first in years). You'll also have more time to devote to pursuits that are fulfilling for you, which will improve your own quality of life.

For adults with developmental disabilities, the biggest benefits of moving out are opportunities for socializing and the chance to learn new things. They meet new people, have new experiences, and are presented with new challenges. These adults often become more social and more independent, and they're also involved in more leisure activities when they move out of the family home. The gains can be small or large. When Ann, age forty, moved into a supported living arrangement with three other women, her mother advised the caregiver that Ann couldn't use a knife or fork. "Generally, I just feed her myself," the mother said. A week later when they met again, the caregiver reported that Ann was already using a fork all the time. After all, the women she lived with did, so Ann wanted to do the same. My daughter Susie discovered Elvis Presley, whose music she loves, when she moved out. This would never have happened if she had continued living at home!

When your adult child moves out of your home, it doesn't mean that you give up all claim to him or her. You can visit your child, just as he or she can visit you, staying for a few days or even longer. The life you share with your child with disabilities will be similar to the life you share with your other adult children: going home to Grandma's for Thanksgiving, going out with the family for Sunday dinner, and so on. You'll still have a large voice in decisions affecting your child, and you'll still be able to advocate for him or her as necessary.

When Is It a Good Time to Move Out?

Finding a good place for your child to live can take anywhere from many months to several years. You must include time for you and your child to visit several potential places, become familiar with whatever option you select together, talk to the people involved, and make your decision. It will also take some time for any needed supports to be put in place. In addition, most good places have a waiting list, so even if you aren't planning for your child to move soon, it's important to get on the waiting list for the placement of your choice.

Special education law requires that schools must begin transition planning for students with a disability when they're sixteen years old and that the students and their parents should be actively involved in this plan. This transition period prepares the student for life after graduation from high school (for example, for a job, post-secondary education, vocational training, or independent living). Students with disabilities are entitled to a public education until age twenty-one, according to federal special education law. Your child's school-related transition planning is a good time for you to begin thinking about his or her future.

You might plan for your son or daughter to move out of your home within a year or so after high school, or you may decide he or she isn't ready yet. Or you may need to base the timing on other criteria, particularly if your child is severely physically disabled. For example, one set of parents decided to look for a good place for their son to live when they realized that soon they wouldn't be able to lift him and transfer him from place to place.

Is Now the Time?

Go back to chapter 2 and look at your assessment of your child's current situation and quality of life. This will give you a good idea about whether now is the time for you to begin planning for your child to move. Also take a look at how you assessed your own quality of life in chapter 2. Remember, you are an important part of the equation. If your quality of life is suffering because caring for your child is physically exhausting or excessively stressful, you should consider having him or her move out. I know this may sound selfish. But remember, you must keep yourself in good shape if you're to be a good parent for the long haul.

You can also turn back to chapter 5, on person-centered planning, and look at your child's interests, strengths, likes, dislikes, and support needs. Your child's person-centered plan can help you decide if now is a good time to consider a move. It can also provide you with ideas on how best to pave the way for a move.

If you've decided that moving out would give your child more opportunities to socialize and more stimulation but you're unsure whether he or she is "ready," ask yourself the following questions:

- Does your child want to move out and live with others who are around the same age?

- If not, is he or she willing to do so?

- Does your child usually wander around the house doing nothing or watch television all day?

- Does he or she generally get along well with others?

- Has your child already spent some time away from you?

- Does he or she cooperate with other caregivers?

Ask other family members and friends what they think, too. Although you probably know your child best, they may be able to give you valuable insight into the situation.

Obviously, there's no set time for your child to move out of the family home. It depends on your situation, and it's a decision to arrive at together with your son or daughter and other family members. But you need to at least start thinking about it now so that you can consider it from all angles and have plenty of time to present the idea and make a well-thought-out plan.

When do you think would be a good time for your son or daughter to move out of the family home? _____

Readiness

You may still think that you need to wait until your child "is ready" before he or she can get a job or move out of your home. You may have been told that your child needs to do something independently before he or she can be allowed to move on to a "higher level." Professionals used to assess the person's readiness to perform more difficult tasks before allowing them to try something out. But if you wait until your child is "ready" to do something or until he or she can do something independently, you may have to wait a long, long time, and along the way he or she will miss some golden opportunities to learn and grow.

Luckily, we don't have to operate on those principles any more. Although your child may always need some support to become a productive adult, no amount of waiting will make him or her "independent" or more "ready." The time is now.

These days, parents are guided by what their adult child with developmental disabilities wants to do. You should assume that your son or daughter can do most things he or she wants to do—with the proper amount and type of support.

Prepare the Way for Your Son or Daughter

When you talk to your son or daughter about moving out, bring up the idea slowly. Point out how others in the family have left home to begin their lives as adults. Be sure you present the move in a positive light. Try to help your child feel enthusiastic about it. Describe it as a new adventure. Stress the fact that he or she will be with friends and will have lots of things to do. Visit others who are living "on their own" so that your child can see what it's like.

Make sure that, to the extent possible, your child is prepared for the responsibilities of living on his or her own or with a small group of people. If your child's living situation will be fairly independent, he or she will need to be familiar with some or even many of the tasks involved in maintaining a household. You may want to review the portions of chapter 4 that discuss the responsibilities that come with adulthood and how you can help your child participate in household tasks. Although your child will continue to learn about these things after he or she has moved out, your child should be as familiar as possible with these tasks and responsibilities before he or she leaves your home.

If your child doesn't want to move out of your home, you can do what the Reynolds family did when it became clear that their son Frank was afraid to leave home. They got Frank involved with a bowling league for people with developmental disabilities, most of them no longer living at home. As the weeks passed, Frank made friends with his teammates, and he and his parents often went out for pizza with them after the game.

Eventually, Frank's parents invited a few of these friends over for dinner, and they, in turn, invited Frank to visit them. When he saw how they lived and how much they were enjoying themselves, Frank was willing to try a sleepover. Soon he was willing to consider moving out of the family home and began to participate in the planning. Although this process took many months, it worked well for Frank. And that made his parents feel better about the move.

It's important to remember that your child may be dependent on you because he or she is isolated from others his or her own age. Getting your child involved with others in the community while he or she is still living at home can help loosen your child's ties to you. Jordan's parents carefully prepared him for moving into a group home in the community, but they were still apprehensive when he moved out. So Jordan's mother picked him up four nights a week and brought him home for dinner. After she had done this for about six weeks, one evening Jordan asked her what she was making for dinner. After she told him, he said he thought he would stay and eat at the group home because he liked what they were having for dinner better.

Prepare Yourself

As you contemplate your son or daughter moving out of your home, prepare yourself for feelings of grief and guilt. When these feelings surface, you have to reassure yourself that you're a good parent and have the best interests of your child at heart. You have a long history of caring, and it won't stop now. You'll be able to see your child as often as you like and assure yourself of his or her well-being.

When your child moves out, your house will feel empty for a while and you may not know what to do with yourself. Take this opportunity to start doing some things for self-enrichment and fun. If you need help getting started on this, look back at chapter 3. If you need support, you can talk to other parents whose son or daughter with developmental disabilities has moved out of the family home. Find out how they felt at the time of the move and how they feel now that time has passed.

Arrange for Support Services

Most adults with developmental disabilities won't be able to live completely independently. You may wonder if enough help will be available to your child so that he or she can get along without your continued care. The answer is yes, but you may have to be very persuasive when discussing this with the community agency. Based on your child's individual needs, community agencies will provide services and supports (including financial support) to enable him or her to live in a situation that suits his or her capabilities. Support services may include help with planning, referrals, coordination of services, counseling, education and training for your son or daughter, and assistance with the tasks of daily living. Supports and services will be specifically designed to accommodate your child's needs.

Generally, families aren't required to contribute money to the upkeep of their adult sons or daughters with developmental disabilities, since various community services agencies and the person's Medicaid and Supplemental Security Income (SSI) or Social Security Disability Insurance (SSDI) generally cover rent, home repairs, salaries for professional caregivers, food, and incidentals. (See chapter 9 for a full discussion of sources of funding.) However, there are, of course, some private living situations where parents are required to pay a large monthly fee.

Review the Person-Centered Plan

Look back at your child's person-centered plan, which you developed in chapter 5, and review the kind and amount of support your child needs for the tasks of daily living. Your child's needs for supports and services depend on his or her capabilities, preferences, and health and safety needs. If your child needs supervision and support twenty-four hours a day, seven days a week, community agencies will provide him or her with what they call 24/7/365 professional caregivers. If your child doesn't need supervision at night, or if he or she only needs a few hours a day of guidance, agencies will provide a part-time caregiver to meet his or her needs. Several residents of an apartment or group living situation can share a caregiver or direct care worker, if feasible. It's important that you have a good idea of the amount of caregiving support you feel your son or daughter needs so that you can discuss this knowledgeably with the agency providing support.

How much support do you think your son or daughter needs? Please check the one answer that seems most applicable:

_____ One-on-one caregiver, twenty-four hours a day

_____ One caregiver for two people, twenty-four hours a day

_____ One caregiver for three to six people, twenty-four hours a day

_____ Only two to three hours a day of supervision or guidance

_____ Only two to four hours a week of supervision or guidance

_____ Other: _____

What sort of living situation would your son or daughter prefer? Find out your son's or daughter's preferences. If he or she can't communicate verbally, you'll have to make an educated guess based on your observations and on input from people who know your son or daughter well. Check all that apply:

_____ Living alone in own apartment, condominium, or house

_____ Sharing a bedroom with one other person

_____ Sharing a home with one other person

_____ Sharing a home with two to five other people

_____ Living with six to sixteen other people

_____ Living in a situation with seventeen or more people

_____ Living near other adults with developmental disabilities

_____ Living with people who don't have disabilities

_____ Remaining in the family home

_____ Other: _____

_____ Other: _____

Options for Living Arrangements

There are many possible living arrangements you can consider for your child, ranging from expensive privately run "villages" to publicly supported living in his or her own apartment. To get an idea of the options available and which of them might be appropriate for your son or daughter, let's take a look at the settings where Jean, Betty, Fred, Scott, Maria, Henry, Mark, Harvey, and CJ live. As you read the descriptions below, visualize your child in each situation, and then answer the questions beneath each. The goal is to consider each situation in light of your child's needs, preferences, and interests to help you decide what sorts of residences might be most appropriate.

Jean: Living in an Apartment of Her Own

Were you to visit Jean, she would proudly show you around her tiny apartment, which she has decorated all in blue. Blue sheets cover her old sofa and chairs, there's a blue bedspread on her bed, and she's painted all the walls blue. About fifteen stuffed animals are piled on her bed, and others are strewn about the apartment. There are even a couple of stuffed animals in the kitchen, tucked into cabinets.

Jean, who is mildly retarded, lives alone and prepares all her own meals, although she does admit to eating a lot of fast food. She works about twenty hours a week and takes a city bus to work and back. Twice a week, a support worker from a community agency visits her for two hours to help her plan her meals for the week, budget her money, and pay her bills. Sometimes they shop for clothes, mostly at resale shops. Her case manager at the community agency monitors her needs.

Jean used to work at a local grocery store before it went out of business. She now has an interim job cleaning offices at the community agency while the agency looks for a new job for her. Jean meets with friends once or twice a week to socialize, and she talks to friends on the telephone almost every day.

Jean's parents are both dead. She occasionally visits her elderly aunt, who lives about sixty miles away. Her support worker arranges for her bus tickets. Jean's expenses are paid by her monthly Supplemental Security Income checks, food stamps, Medicaid, and Section 8 rent support. (See chapter 9 for details on these sources of funding.)

Would your son or daughter like to live in his or her own apartment?   Yes No

Is this a good situation for your son or daughter?   Yes   No

Is Jean's level of support appropriate for your son or daughter?   Yes   No

What are the pros and cons of this arrangement for your son or daughter?

Pros   **Cons**

_____   _____

_____   _____

_____   _____

_____   _____

_____   _____

Betty: Living in a Village

If you were to visit Betty, you would think you'd died and gone to heaven. First of all, you drive through the beautiful Virginia hills to get there. Then, down a dirt road and around a bend, you glimpse Innisfree, a "village" nestled in a valley. Innisfree consists of a number of houses resembling summer cottages set in the woods, a large farm with a barn for the animals, and several separate buildings housing a bakery, a woodworking shop, a weaving workshop, and central administration buildings. There are about forty residents in the village.

Betty has her own room, as do all the residents. She shares her house with three to four other residents. A volunteer lives in each house, acting more like a trusted friend than a caregiver and exercising minimal supervision over the residents. This village is the Rolls-Royce of residential facilities for adults with mild disabilities. There are similar villages around the country, such as Camphill and New England Villages. Needless to say, the cost to the family is quite high (ranging from $25,000 to $50,000 a year), although Social Security and Medicaid help offset some expenses, providing about $8,000 per year.

Betty has become a talented weaver and sells the textiles she produces at the village store. (I recently had dinner with her mother, and the table was set with napkins Betty had woven by hand.) She also volunteers once a week at a day care facility in a nearby town. She's able to take a plane by herself to visit her mother in the Midwest several times a year for a week at a time. In addition, her mother drives to Virginia to visit Betty twice a year and stays at the village for a few days. Her father also visits her from his home in California.

Would your son or daughter like to live in a village?   Yes   No

Is this a good situation for your son or daughter?   Yes   No

Is Betty's level of support appropriate for your son or daughter?   Yes   No

What are the pros and cons of this arrangement for your son or daughter?

Pros   **Cons**

_____   _____

_____   _____

_____ _____
_____ _____
_____ _____

Fred: Living in a Rented House

Fred lives with two other young men in a rented house near the center of a small town. The house belongs to a philanthropic group formed for the specific purpose of purchasing housing for people with autism. A brick ranch house built in the 1950s, their home has three bedrooms and a finished belowground basement. The parents of the three young men furnished the house with spare furniture from their own homes along with furnishings contributed by friends. Each of the young men has his own bedroom. Fred's is neat and his bed is made, and the other two bedrooms have that casual, lived-in look.

Fred and his housemates have one direct care worker during the day and a live-in house manager at night, who sleeps in the basement. They need this level of support because each young man has both physical and mental impairments. Fred's impairments are autism and mild to moderate mental retardation. Fred's two housemates, who are legally blind as well as mildly mentally impaired, can take a city bus by themselves if they don't have to cross the street to get it or change buses. Otherwise, the men take a special taxi that costs them two dollars each way. With caregiver support, the three of them shop, go to the movies, eat out, and prepare their own meals. Once a week, Fred and his housemates attend Friendship Fellowship in the evening, a church-sponsored group with a mission to serve people with developmental disabilities. One of their direct care workers drives them there and back.

They receive half of their rent money from Section 8 rent assistance, which provides federal housing money for the elderly, those with low incomes, and people with disabilities. The provisions of Section 8 require that the house be inspected once a year. Otherwise the house doesn't have to meet the licensing requirements of a group home or adult foster care facility because the house is considered a family home in which three unrelated adults live. Fred's other living expenses are covered by his SSI, food stamps, and Medicaid. The community agency pays for Fred's professional caregivers.

Would your son or daughter like to live in a rented house with several housemates?   Yes   No

Is this a good situation for your son or daughter?   Yes   No

Is Fred's level of support appropriate for your son or daughter?   Yes   No

What are the pros and cons of this arrangement for your son or daughter?

Pros   Cons

_____   _____

_____   _____

_____   _____

_____   _____

_____   _____

Scott: Living in a Group Home

Scott lives in a large ranch-style brick house on a large lot with a paved walkway for wheelchair users. Built in the 1980s by a community agency, the house was designed specifically for people using wheelchairs. Scott lives with two men and three women, who are all physically and mentally impaired and have medical problems as well. The family room of the house, complete with a large fish tank and lava lamps to catch the eye, is used as an activity center. Scott especially enjoys going for a walk in the neighborhood or sitting outside on the large paved patio when the weather is warm, and he gets quite grumpy when it's too cold for this.

Scott needs some type of assistance with nearly everything he does. Because the residents' needs are so great, the staff ratio in their group home is one direct care worker to two residents. Scott's day begins around 6:00 a.m., when he and his housemates get up and their caregivers begin the long process of getting everyone ready for the day. During the week Scott goes to school from 9:00 a.m. to 2:30 p.m. When he returns home, he takes a nap, has dinner with his housemates, and takes a shower before going to bed at 9:00 p.m. Some weekends a direct care worker takes Scott and another resident to the mall to just hang out. Occasionally they go to the nature center, a movie, or a museum. The caregivers provide all transportation, prepare all meals, and do the cleaning. Scott's parents, who live in the same town, drop in about once a week to visit him and monitor the services he's receiving.

Unfortunately, many adults with severe developmental disabilities are placed in nursing homes where they have little in common with the elderly residents and receive no training and little stimulation. But in reality, adults like Scott, with severe multiple needs, can be served much better in small community settings with staff specifically trained to both respond to their needs and provide maximum community integration. Scott's living expenses are paid by SSI, food stamps, and Medicaid. A community agency pays for the staff.

Would your son or daughter like to live in a group home with a small group of other housemates?   Yes   No

Is this a good situation for your son or daughter?   Yes   No

Is Scott's level of support appropriate for your son or daughter?   Yes   No

What are the pros and cons of this arrangement for your son or daughter?

Pros   **Cons**

_____   _____

_____   _____

_____   _____

_____   _____

_____   _____

Maria: Living in a Church-Run Residential Center

Many private residential facilities are run by churches. The Catholic Church, for example, has several residential facilities scattered around the United States for people with mild to severe cognitive impairments or mental retardation, including mild physical or neurological disabilities. Other denominations also have residential facilities, and most of these residences accept people of other faiths. These facilities often serve twenty to seventy residents, and as such fall into the category that state agencies generally refer to as "intermediate care facilities."

Many of these facilities are on large tracts of farmland in the country. Residents live in apartments or houses in groups of six to eight in a campuslike setting. Several of these church-run facilities are willing to accept SSI, SSDI, Food Stamps, and Medicaid as the only financial requirement and rely on donations and fund-raising to help meet their budgets. Many community agencies pay for staffing at this type of facility, although some don't. These facilities must meet state and local health and safety requirements for the residents to receive financial support from state and community agencies.

The Saint Louis Center, where Maria lives, is located on 150 acres of rolling farmland near a small town. She lives with four to seven other young women in an apartment with four double bedrooms, a large living room, a kitchen, a dining room, and an office for staff. Currently Maria has her own room, but she'd rather have a roommate.

Attached is another apartment that currently houses seven young men in a mirror-image setting. The residents often go back and forth between the apartments for barbecues, bingo, or just to socialize. Each apartment has full-time, round-the-clock staff. Also on the grounds is another similar building with two apartments and a large central administration building with another apartment. The large central building also includes a chapel, a gym, a large commercial kitchen, a dining room, and offices for the staff.

Maria can go to the other apartments, the office, the chapel, and the kitchen without supervision—something she couldn't do if she lived in town. Most of the adult residents go out into nearby communities to work, take classes, shop, or go to the movies. Transportation is provided by the center staff and by community agencies. Like the other residents, Maria is required to visit her family every other weekend and for four weeklong vacations a year; however, residents who have no family stay at the facility all the time.

Would your son or daughter like to live in a church-run residential center? Yes No

Is this a good situation for your son or daughter? Yes No

Is Maria's level of support appropriate for your son or daughter? Yes No

What are the pros and cons of this arrangement for your son or daughter?

Pros   **Cons**

_____   _____

_____   _____

_____   _____

_____   _____

_____   _____

Henry: Living with a Foster Family

Henry has lived with a foster family for many years, ever since his mother had an emotional breakdown and his parents got a divorce. His foster family, which has an adult foster care license, cares for Henry and one other adult with developmental disabilities in their home. A community agency helped locate the foster family and, along with Henry's SSI, pays for his upkeep.

Henry has truly become part of his foster family. He attends church with them and goes on all family outings. He also attends a day activity center, with transportation there and back provided by a community agency. His foster family is poor and Henry's room is modest, but the house is neat and clean and Henry is quite happy there.

Henry's entire family lives out of town—both of his parents and his brother and sister. Henry's father and older brother try to visit him once a month, and although he isn't required to do so, his father contributes money to the family from time to time.

Would your son or daughter like to live with a foster family?   Yes   No

Is this a good situation for your son or daughter?   Yes   No

Is Henry's level of support appropriate for your son or daughter?   Yes   No

What are the pros and cons of this arrangement for your son or daughter?

Pros   **Cons**

_____   _____

_____   _____

_____   _____

_____   _____

_____   _____

Mark and Harvey: Sharing a Condominium

Mark and Harvey live in a condominium in the city purchased by their parents. Each has his own bedroom. A direct care worker visits them twice a day, once in the morning to help them get started on their day and once in the early evening to help them prepare for the next day and iron out any problems they might have had. Both men work about twenty hours a week and take the bus to work. Mark's expenses are paid by SSI, food stamps, Section 8 rent support, and Medicaid. Both men pay rent to their parents, who own the condominium. A community agency pays for the direct care worker Mark and Harvey share.

Mark's mother picks him up on Sundays to attend church and on Tuesday evenings to take him to swimming at the Y. On Thursday evenings, Mark takes a reduced-fare taxi to go to Friendship Fellowship, which meets at the Christian Reformed Church. Harvey stays home both evenings to watch television, his favorite occupation. There are three other adults with developmental disabilities living in the condominium complex. They all often get together around the pool, and they meet once a week for dinner at each other's condo (most of the time their parents do the cooking).

Would your son or daughter like to share a condo or apartment with another person?   Yes   No

Is this a good situation for your son or daughter?   Yes   No

Is Mark and Harvey's level of support appropriate for your son or daughter? Yes   No

What are the pros and cons of this arrangement for your son or daughter?

Pros   **Cons**

_____   _____

_____   _____

_____   _____

_____   _____

_____   _____

CJ: Living with His Family

CJ, who is twenty-eight years old, lives with his large family in an old house at the edge of town. He has an older brother and sister, both of whom are married and have babies, and two younger sisters. They are all very close in age. Although his older brother and sister live in their own homes nearby, they are often at their parent's house for dinner or for a splash in the aboveground pool in the summertime. CJ often goes to the movies and sports events with one or another of his siblings.

CJ works with his mother cleaning houses. He occasionally complains about his mother always telling him what to do, but he has no desire to move out of the family home at this time and his parents are happy to have him there. He receives no services or funding from community agencies, but he does receive SSI (at a reduced rate because he's living at home).

Would your son or daughter like to live at home with your family?   Yes   No

Is this a good situation for your son or daughter?   Yes   No

Is CJ's level of support appropriate for your son or daughter?   Yes   No

What are the pros and cons of this arrangement for your son or daughter?

Pros   Cons

_____   _____

_____   _____

_____   _____

_____   _____

_____   _____

Visualize the Ideal Living Situation

Now that you've read the descriptions of various types of residential situations, try to visualize the ideal situation for your son or daughter. If none of the above arrangements seem suitable for your son or daughter, try to come up with a situation that does. Describe it: _____

_____

_____

_____

Now describe the amount of staff support your son or daughter will need in order to live there: _____

_____

_____

_____

Additional Factors to Consider

Once you've chosen the type of residential situation that seems appropriate, there are many other factors to consider before choosing the specific place where your child will live. Here are some of the sorts of things you need to think about:

■   Location

- The physical building: layout, accessibility, number of bathrooms, and so on

- The philosophy of the agency running the house

- Whether potential housemates or roommates are compatible

- What work arrangements and daytime activities are available to the residents

- The training, experience, and personality of the direct care workers

- The amount and type of support services available

- Transportation

- Available funding

Work opportunities, meaningful activities, direct care workers, support services, and funding will all be covered in depth in chapters 7 through 9, so for now, let's take a closer look at location, the building itself, potential housemates and roommates, and the facility's guiding philosophy.

Location

The first thing you need to consider is the location of the residence. You may have more than one location in mind. For example, Mark's parents wanted him to live within a half-hour drive of their home so they could take him to various activities. They drew a circle on a map that encompasses everything within a half hour of their home and narrowed their search accordingly.

Recently, a community agency offered to move Mark from his condo to a large house in a neighboring community. Well-built and well-furnished, it was in an upper-middle-class neighborhood and had a large yard with wonderful landscaping. But it was on the edge of town, away from anything of interest to Mark and away from a bus line. Mark and his parents decided against it, even though the house was much nicer than the condo he lives in with Harvey.

Your child may want to live in the heart of town, where he or she can walk to stores and restaurants. If your child is able to take the bus to work and to other activities, you may want him or her to live near a bus stop. Or you may want your child to live in a more protected environment—on a farm, for example.

Where would your son or daughter prefer to live, and what sort of location would work well for you? Check all options that apply.

_____ In a city

_____ In a small town

_____ On a farm or in a rural setting

_____ Within walking distance of shopping and other activities

_____ Near public transportation

_____ Near me or another family member

_____ In our family home (at least for the next few years)

_____ Other: _____

_____ Other: _____

Most adults with developmental disabilities would probably prefer to live near a family member, or at least in a location where a family member can visit frequently. If you're planning for the time when you may not be around, this may mean that your child needs to move to another state to be near a sibling or other family member.

Moving to a Different State

If moving to another state is a possibility for your child, but you don't have a particular situation in mind, you can contact that state's agency responsible for people with developmental disabilities to find out what type of housing and support services are offered in that state and how eligibility and residency are established. Generally, community agencies won't provide support services to people who aren't residents of their state or locality. Services from the state where your child formerly resided will cease as soon as he or she leaves that state with the intention to relocate. This can mean a potential gap of three to six months or more in publicly funded services if your child moves from one state to another. Creative planning and strong advocacy on your part can help keep this gap to the minimum.

If you decide that your child will be moving to another state, contact that state's department of developmental disabilities right away to get the intake process going. You'll have to fill out an application for the particular region or county in which your son or daughter will reside. You can send the agency your child's current person-centered plan and service plan and any recent evaluations. You should also arrange to visit the community agency in the new state with your child so that the agency can interview him or her. Doing this well in advance of the move will give the community agency time for determining eligibility (which can take two to three months). Only when your child actually moves to that state will the agency begin looking for a potential residence for him or her.

The Physical Building

If a community agency has located a residence for you to inspect, you need to find out if the facility is fully licensed; otherwise, make sure it has passed any required inspections. It should also be in good repair and be located in a safe neighborhood. Here are some other things you'll probably want to consider:

- Is the level of cleanliness acceptable?

- Is it in good repair?

- If stairs are a problem for your child, are all rooms on one floor?

- Is the number of bathrooms adequate and are there grab bars in the bathrooms, if needed?

- Is it adequately furnished?

- Is the yard fenced?

The Program and Guiding Philosophy

Once again, a beautiful, well-furnished residence in a safe neighborhood isn't enough. What goes on inside the residence is probably a lot more important to your child. Sitting around all day doing nothing is not what a good life is all about. Meaningful activity and satisfying interactions with others are the cornerstone of a good residential situation. The residence and its guiding philosophy should provide a setting that will encourage your child to be busy and productive.

A residential situation need not have a formalized program per se, but there should be a guiding philosophy. Person-centered planning (or something similar) should be a part of this guiding philosophy. This means that day-to-day decisions and activities depend on the preferences and interests of the people who live in the residence and are individualized based on abilities and needs.

Some residences for adults with developmental disabilities are sponsored by churches and other faith-based organizations. As part of their guiding philosophy, these facilities often follow the tenets of a particular religious faith. However, they generally do welcome people of other faiths as residents.

Some aspects of a residence's programs and philosophy are easily observed. Don't hesitate to ask about others. Here are some things you can look for:

- Areas for playing games or pursuing hobbies

- A calendar with a list of daily activities and upcoming events displayed prominently

- Residents appropriately dressed

- Residents busy cooking, cleaning, and so forth

- Volunteers from the community in evidence

Here are some things you'll probably need to ask about:

- What does each resident do during the day on a typical day?

- How often does each resident get out into the community?

- How often do residents get together with other friends?

- Does each resident have an individualized plan? Are activities individualized?

- Are pets allowed?

- Do they welcome parent involvement?

A Homelike Atmosphere

The place where your child lives doesn't need to look like your home, but it needs to feel like home. The décor can be either old-fashioned or modern and the furniture can be mismatched and even a bit shabby, but the residence needs to look warm, inviting, and lived-in. Far too many residential situations for adults with developmental disabilities look institutional. They often have plastic furniture covers, bare floors, artificial plants, and nothing out of place. This isn't what a home should look like, no matter how convenient it is to keep up.

A home is colorful and may have live houseplants. Housemates' personal articles are in evidence, and the smell of good cooking wafts through the air. Residents are often involved in housekeeping or other personal tasks. Laughter, conversation, and music fill the air, and the TV provides only occasional entertainment. Pets, whether goldfish, cats, or dogs, are usually a welcome addition, providing a source of affection and engagement.

When you're visiting different residences, here are some things to look for in bedrooms:

- Posters and pictures on walls that are appropriate for adults

- Popular music tapes and CDs that reflect individual preferences

- Places for residents to display artwork, photographs, notes, and the like

■ Individualized décor, such as favorite pillows, chairs, or bedding

A Supportive Environment

Other, more subtle qualities contribute to a supportive environment for adults with developmental disabilities, including positive expectations, a sense of belonging among residents, team spirit, and a sense of fun. It is largely the direct care worker who assures that the residential situation has these qualities.

These subtle qualities often can only be observed over time, which means that you and your child need to visit any residential situation you're considering several times before making a decision. In addition, your child may want to visit for a long weekend or two to experience all that the situation has to offer. If a community agency is in charge of the residence you want to visit, you'll need to make arrangements through that agency. You can make arrangements to visit a private or church-run residence directly.

Housemates or Roommates

If your son or daughter is going to live alone, you won't have to worry about housemates or roommates. However, if your child will be living with others, try to make sure that the other residents will be compatible with him or her. If the community agency knows the other residents, they can help you decide whether your child will get along well with them. While your own first impressions are important, long-term compatibility is hard to determine without knowing all the residents well.

It doesn't matter whether all the residents have the same type of disability. Nor is it important whether they're all the same age. It is important, however, that residents have compatible abilities and disabilities; this will allow them to help each other. If adequate supervision and privacy is maintained, they need not all be of the same sex. Your son or daughter might enjoy living in a house with members of the opposite sex.

Find Out What's Available

Once you've zeroed in on the kind of living situation and the general location that you think would suit your child, it's time to begin looking at specific living situations in the town or county of your choice. Local, county, or regional community agencies can inform you of the options that exist nearby. They can make suggestions to help you in your search. They also maintain waiting lists for local housing, so it's important that you contact them early in your search. They should be able to tell you which residences have openings and possibly give you an idea of how long the wait will be for openings at other residences. As new openings arise, the community agency will inform you of their availability. You and your child will be able to visit the residence before making up your mind. You'll also be able to meet the other residents and the caregivers.

Don't let the options suggested by a community agency limit you. For various reasons, community agencies may not suggest all the options that exist in the location you're considering. For example, they usually don't suggest private, church-run, or intermediate care facilities. If you're thinking of a private placement, similar to the village where Betty lives and the church-run facility where Maria lives, use the Internet to identify different options and get more information about them. You can ask other parents and parent organizations, such as the Arc and United Cerebral Palsy, for names and locations of private residential situations. You can also contact various faith-based groups to find out where their residential facilities are located and get more information about those facilities.

What to Do If Your First Choice Doesn't Work Out

Your goal is to find a more or less permanent place for your child to call home. However, it's entirely possible that the first place he or she moves to may not work out. There may be problems with other residents, with direct care workers, or with a lack of activities that had been promised. Don't bring your child home at the first sign of a problem; try to work it out. You can meet with the case worker provided by your community agency, the families of other residents, direct care workers, and other staff members to help you resolve the problem.

In the process, try not to blame or personally attack any particular person. These situations usually arise due to system problems, such as lack of training or poor planning, and making the needed changes often requires long-term advocacy on the part of parents and advocacy organizations. That said, sometimes problems with a particular direct care worker can't be resolved, and it may be necessary to change either the caregiver or a service provider. Your community agency case worker will help you with this.

Create Your Own Options

If no openings exist in the living situation of your choice or if nothing you find seems satisfactory, consider creating a living situation for your child. You might buy a house together with several other families—perhaps members of the same organization for families of people with developmental disabilities, or perhaps families you met at a school your child attended. These families can form a nonprofit organization to access funding from federal and state housing programs. For example, Section 811 of the Housing Act of 1959 can provide low-interest loans to nonprofit organizations. Another option is to try to locate a philanthropic organization willing to buy a house that they'd rent to several adults with developmental disabilities. That's what Fred's mother did, after much research on the Internet.

One woman bought a house near a university and rented rooms to college students at a reduced rate in exchange for spending some time with her son in the afternoon and being available at night should her son need help. During the day, her son receives support services from a community agency and works part-time. To give you more ideas about how this might work, let's take a closer look at the living situations created by several different families.

The House That Pat Built

A few years ago at an outing for young people with developmental disabilities sponsored by the local chapter of Alhambra, a nationwide fraternal organization, Pat found himself talking with one of the volunteers about his dream of building a home for his daughter Lexi and a few of her friends. The volunteer from Alhambra said, "Funny, at our last meeting, we were talking about doing something just like that."

Over the next several months, Pat attended several Alhambra meetings to discuss the idea, and soon the group decided to proceed with the project. They had enough money in their treasury to build the house, so the next step was finding an affordable piece of property in a good location. It took them three years to find the right property in a small, quiet subdivision. The builder, also a member of Alhambra, was ready to go ahead as soon as they acquired the property, and the house was built in a mere three months.

Light and airy, it's a modest house with four bedrooms, two full baths, a living room, a family room, and a porch that looks out on the backyard. The house was designed to be easily converted into a family home should it be sold in the future. The builder built the house at cost, and half the cost of materials and labor was donated. Pat, a retired teacher, got a builder's license, and he and another father of a potential resident corralled friends to help with the construction. Led by Pat's wife, Barb, the mothers worked on fund-raising. They sent out letters to everyone they could think of asking for donations to Alhambra for the project and netted $40,000. All the furnishings of the house were donated by family and friends.

The house is owned by the Manresa chapter of Alhambra, and members of Alhambra will continue to maintain the house. The four young women now living in the house pay the rent out of their SSI checks, but the amount isn't enough to cover the full cost of maintaining the house, so Alhambra must make up the difference each month. Alhambra is currently seeking tax abatement for the house.

Because the house doesn't need an adult foster care license, it only had to pass the inspections the city requires for all residential construction. Pat was careful to include the local community agency in the planning process so that the house would meet their requirements. The agency pays for a house manager and 24/7/365 staff, including "awake" staff at night since two of the women have seizures that aren't completely controlled.

Kindred Spirit

In Clio, Michigan, the Montagues built a state-of-the-art group home for their son with severe cerebral palsy and several of his friends with various disabilities. Called Kindred Spirit, the 15,000-square-foot home can accommodate up to twelve residents and includes a three-bedroom apartment for a live-in house manager plus two individual rooms where parents of residents can stay for several days at a time. This is especially useful when parents are helping their son or daughter adjust to moving out of the family home. During those few days, parents show the staff techniques and strategies they've used to help their son or daughter with daily routines.

The house is large yet very homey, with carpeted floors, plants, and a large fish tank in the wide hallway. There are lifts in the ceilings of some of the rooms that enable a person with cerebral palsy to get out of bed and into the bathroom (with the help of a direct care worker). Everything about the house is informed by the Montagues' experiences as parents of a son with developmental disabilities. The staff is very supportive of parents as well.

The adults who live at Kindred Spirit pay nothing beyond their SSI or SSDI. The local community agency, with additional funding from Medicaid, pays for the services and supports each resident needs. Although the Montagues paid for the building itself, all appliances and furnishings were donated by local businesses, and much of the labor was donated as well. The Montagues also pay an hourly supplement to the direct care workers' basic wage because, as business people, they know you get what you pay for.

Intentional Community

About forty families in one small city have gotten together to plan one or more small communities where their sons and daughters can live near each other and get together informally with friends on a daily basis. Intentional community is a good answer to the isolation adults with developmental disabilities often feel when living in scattered sites in the community. These intentional communities will be similar to cohousing communities and the senior citizen communities that are springing up all over the country. The dream is that there will be individual apartments or condominiums as well as three- or four-bedroom houses with space for live-in staff. There will be a large community gathering place for dining and other activities.

These intentional communities are in the planning stage right now, but the directors have met with the local community agency to get their guidance and approval and ensure that needed services and supports will be available to the residents. They've also met with city and county officials to help them locate affordable land that's on a bus line and near stores and restaurants. They may buy a piece of existing housing stock (apartments or condos) to establish their community.

If you plan to build or buy a house, be sure to involve the community agency that will provide supports for your child so that the residence will meet their approval. The agency will usually pay for staffing the house, but only if it meets their requirements. If more than four unrelated adults will be living in the house, it will probably have to meet certain licensing requirements, too. Some of the agencies that may require licensing are the federal government (for Section 8 rent support), your local fire department (for fire safety), your state social services agency (if adult foster care licensing is necessary, there may be requirements for bedroom square footage, number of bathrooms, and so on), or your local housing agency (there may be a limit on the number of unrelated adults who can share a house in a particular neighborhood). Don't buy a house unless any repairs or renovations required are within your budget. You may need to build a new bathroom, for example, and this could be quite costly.

If you buy a house, you can arrange for the other residents who share the house with your child to pay you a reasonable amount of rent to offset your expenses. To locate additional sources of funding, use your local library or the Internet to research philanthropic organizations, granting agencies, and foundations. The Arc and United Cerebral Palsy are also sources of information in this regard. Another excellent resource is *Regional Housing Forum: A Technical Assistance Guide for Housing Resources and Strategies* (Cooper and O'Hara 2003).

At this point in the planning process, what sort of living situation seems to meet the needs and preferences of your adult child with developmental disabilities? Please describe it here, and feel free to describe more than one situation:

_____

_____

_____

_____

_____

_____

Next Steps

Choosing where and with whom your child will live probably feels like the most critical decision you face in planning for his or her future. It's important to remember that the best overall living situation for your child isn't just a particular house or a particular location. You must also take into account the guiding philosophy and program of activities, the kinds of work situations or day programs that will be available to your child (covered in chapter 7), and the training and experience of the caregivers who will provide needed supports and services (covered in chapter 8). Of course, how well your child gets along with other residents is important too.

As is so often the case, these decisions are seldom a choice between what is obviously good and what is obviously bad. The ideal residence, job, or caregiver rarely exists; more often you must choose an option that's the best one available under the circumstances (and then try to make it better). But if you take the time to consider all the options and plan carefully, you can rest assured that your child will be able to live in a warm and supportive atmosphere.

CHAPTER 7

Building a Busy and Productive Life

A good place to live involves more than just the location of a house and its physical features. It includes what goes on inside the house, the programs, the people who share the house, and the caregivers. It also includes access to a busy and productive life.

The previous chapter explored the types of residential situations available and helped you think about which options might best suit your son or daughter, but to come up with the best living situation, you'll need to explore further. You need to make sure that your child has meaningful activities in his or her daily life, whether that means work, education, volunteering, or recreational activities. Sitting at home day after day watching television is not the recipe for a satisfactory life—no matter how beautiful the setting or how wonderful the caregivers.

There has been a lot of research on the isolation and loneliness of adults with developmental disabilities. Much of their isolation is due to the fact that few of them have jobs or are involved in other meaningful activities. Less than one-third of these adults are working either full-time or part-time (NOD/Harris Survey 2004). Two-thirds of those who aren't working want to work (NOD/Harris Survey 2000). For adults with a greater degree of cognitive or intellectual disability, the statistics are more disheartening: 90 percent are unemployed (Rizzolo et al. 2004).

This chapter will provide you with information about different types of work opportunities and other meaningful activities your adult child can become involved in. It will help you create a busy and productive life for your child, based on his or her interests and needs.

A New World of Possibilities

We've come a long way in the past forty years in our thinking about what people with developmental disabilities can and cannot do. Not only have we found out that children with developmental disabilities can learn and prosper in public schools, we've also discovered that adults with developmental disabilities can work at a variety of jobs and often make excellent employees. Employers report that they work hard, come to work on time, and are rarely absent. Provided with the appropriate support services by community and provider agencies, adults with developmental disabilities can now work at jobs in the community alongside nondisabled people.

Yet when asked whether we want our sons and daughters to have a job, many of us merely say "I just want my child to be happy," regardless of the fact that being employed can make a large contribution to that happiness (NOD/Harris Survey 2000). Most of us can't imagine what our sons and daughters could do in terms of work. And, of course, people in general usually have difficulty imagining a person with developmental disabilities holding down a job. Although more adults with developmental disabilities are working than ever before, employers and other employees often have to be sold on the idea that these people can make a genuine contribution to a business or company.

> Take some time to think about how your adult child with developmental disabilities spends his or her day. Is your son or daughter busy or engaged in some activity most of the time?   Yes   No
>
> Is your son or daughter involved in what's going on around him or her to some extent?   Yes   No
>
> Do you think he or she is satisfied with the amount of activity available? Yes   No
>
> Please explain: _____
>
> _____
>
> _____

Consider whether living in a nice home is enough to make your child happy. Is being well cared for enough? Or does your child, like the rest of us, need something meaningful to be occupied with, something interesting to be engaged in, something valuable to strive for, in order to feel satisfied with life?

You may never have thought that work could be an important part of your child's sense of well-being. I certainly never did. Boy, was I wrong! Susie began to work more than fifteen years ago, when she was twenty-six years old and about to graduate from school. Sister Theresa, with the prodding of Sister Joanne, had recently begun the first sheltered workshop at Our Lady of Providence Center (see "Sheltered Workshops," later in this chapter). Sister Theresa, Susie, and I were having our annual meeting regarding Susie's program. I tentatively brought up the idea of Susie working in the workshop, not having any idea of what Susie could do. Sister Theresa was willing to discuss it. She looked at Susie and asked her if she would like to work. Susie's eyes lit up, and she nodded her head with a vigorous yes. Sister Theresa laughed and said, "Let's try it! We can bring one of the jobs upstairs to Susie's classroom and teach her there. If that works, we can try her in the workshop. Okay, Susie?" Susie's smile lit up the room.

It really was a gamble on Sister Theresa's part. Among other things, Susie drooled and we weren't sure how Sister Joanne would handle that. But we tried it anyway. Susie was very motivated and worked hard to learn the steps of the job, which involved putting together small parts to be used in manufacturing washing machines. She did well, so they moved her to the workshop. On her first day of work, Sister Joanne asked Susie if she could stop drooling. She carefully explained that drooling could ruin the work. She told Susie to try to swallow if she felt herself drooling. Needless to say, we had tried for many years to figure out a way to stop Susie from drooling, with no success. Susie loved that job so much that she stopped drooling within one week!

About a month after she started working, Susie greeted me with "Look Ma, pay-check!" She continued, "Put on refrigerator." "Where does it go?" I asked. "Bank," she said somewhat dispiritedly. "I'll tell you what," I said. "I'll make you a copy to put on the refrigerator, and then we can deposit the check in the bank."

Susie is extremely proud of working. Work has gotten her through some rough times, such as when Our Lady of Providence Center closed and she had to adjust to new surroundings and new people. The sense of accomplishment that she got from her new work program helped her overcome the anxiety she felt at making the move to a new residence. Her gifted employment support workers, Andrea and Irma, saw to it that Susie was appropriately challenged and then rewarded for her hard work, and this made Susie feel good about herself even when she was chastised for not following the rules in her new residence.

Susie recently told me that she had gotten an award at work, "I get award. Bring home show Mom." When she brought it home, I copied it, and then I framed the original and gave it to her and hung the copy up in my office.

The Importance of Work

We tend to think that people work solely to support themselves financially, but work also brings friendships, laughter, a chance to learn new things, and feelings of competence and pride. Work gives structure and a sense of purpose to the day and provides opportunities to be productive and helpful. Work is an important part of a person's adult identity, and this is as true for people with developmental disabilities as it is for the rest of us. Working at a job we like greatly increases our life satisfaction.

Research has shown that people with developmental disabilities like to work (NOD/Harris Survey 2000). They like getting paid and they make friends on the job. Many of them say they would feel bad, bored, or lonely if they didn't have a job.

The importance of work for people with disabilities was recognized by Congress in the Statement of Findings introducing the Rehabilitation Act of 1973: "Work is a valued activity, both for individuals and society. [Work] fulfills the need of an individual to be productive, promotes independence, enhances self-esteem, and allows for participation in the mainstream of life in the United States."

When I was looking for a place for Susie to live after Our Lady of Providence closed, it was clear to me that the most important aspect of a living situation for her was that it include access to a job. A private agency in a nearby community showed me a beautiful house in an upper-middle-class suburb, but when I asked them about transportation to a job, they told me it wasn't included—and even if it were, there were no jobs nearby. As nice as the house was, I turned it down.

Employment Support Services

It may be hard for you to imagine your child working if your vision is of him or her working alone in the rough-and-tumble atmosphere of the average job. In actuality, community and provider agencies will provide your child with the support he or she needs to succeed in a job. Work settings can vary from sheltered workshops with full-time staff to mainstream jobs supported by a job coach. So replace any fears with a vision of your child with a support provider at his or her side, explaining and demonstrating the duties of the job and keeping him or her on track.

Most communities have provider agencies, private nonprofit agencies that provide comprehensive employment support services to adults with disabilities. The intensity of these support services depends on the needs of the individual. Local community agencies have lists of providers from which your child can choose. The provider agencies are paid by the community agency.

Your state department of Vocational Rehabilitation Services (VRS), a publicly funded agency, can provide referrals, job and career counseling, training, and job placement services. Look up "Vocational Rehabilitation Services" in the state government pages in your phone book. These agencies can employ job coaches, site managers, and support staff to provide the services a person with disabilities needs to perform a job successfully. VRS can also channel funding to community service providers.

Job Coaches

A job coach helps the person with developmental disabilities find a job, identifies the types of assistance he or she needs, teaches the person the skills necessary to successfully perform the job, and provides on-the-job support. A job coach will generally work one on one with the person, especially if he or she is the only worker with a disability at that site. Job coaches also ensure that transportation to and from the job site is available and train the person on how to travel in the community alone, if appropriate.

Before your child actually starts on the job, his or her job coach will take him or her around the work site, introducing your child to the other workers and familiarizing him or her with the location of the bathroom, telephone, break room, and so on. Then the job coach will familiarize your child with work-related routines, such as punching the time clock or putting things away when not in use.

The job coach will break the job down into steps before the first day of work. Each step is taught or demonstrated separately, with plenty of time for your child to practice each step. Then the job coach works alongside him or her, modeling the work. Next, the job coach sits back and watches while your child does the job alone, cueing him or her if he or she forgets something. The job coach will go to work with your child for several weeks or even a month or so to ensure that he or she has learned the job adequately.

The job coach slowly withdraws support once your child is ready but will continue to check on him or her from time to time. In addition, both your child and the employer or supervisor will have the job coach's phone number so they can get in contact at a moment's notice. With the aid of a job coach, many adults with developmental disabilities can work in neighborhood businesses, allowing them to move from sheltered work settings into more integrated and natural situations.

Job coaches can also locate potential work sites for their clients. They analyze companies to identify the best match between a business and potential workers. They work with the potential employer to figure out how the potential employee can do a particular job, assessing what modifications may be needed and what support the job coach should supply. Needless to say, job coaches often have to persuade the employer to take a chance on the employee.

One of a job coach's major duties is to train and support employers and coworkers on how to best work with the person with developmental disabilities. The state vocational rehabilitation services agency and the state department of labor also provide training for both employers and workers with disabilities. The federal Job Training Partnership Act calls for reimbursing employers of people with disabilities up to half of their salary for a period of six months. Certain tax credits are available for employers, as well.

Site Managers

The site manager's responsibilities are similar to those of the job coach. Site managers oversee small groups of adults who work in more sheltered environments in the community, such as enclaves, sheltered workshops, and community experience programs. The work they supervise can be either paid or volunteer

A work group may focus on only one job or may have several jobs alternating during the week. Often the jobs are located at different sites. As the work group moves from site to site in the community, the group members expand their community experiences.

Job Modifications and Accommodations

When you begin to think of possible jobs for your son or daughter, you may think, "If only such-and-such wasn't such a busy, noisy place" or "If only my son didn't have to work so fast" or "If only my daughter could work a few hours in the morning, when she isn't so tired."

The Americans with Disabilities Act specifies that people with disabilities are entitled to reasonable work accommodations and modifications if they are otherwise capable of doing a certain job. "Reasonable" usually means the accommodation isn't too costly and doesn't affect the quality of the work or the product being manufactured.

Often a slight change in the way a job is done or an exchange of a few tasks from one person to another can help make a job easier and thus make it possible. A job coach, working with the employer, is trained to develop modifications and accommodations that will enable adults with developmental disabilities to successfully perform their jobs. Here are some examples of job modifications and accommodations that have been implemented by employers:

- Allowing the person with disabilities to work during nonpeak hours: This can certainly help those who are affected by noise and chaos or who can't work as fast.

- Providing a separate room in which to work: This can help those who are easily distracted.

- Arranging a part-time schedule for a person who has difficulty working a full eight-hour day: Modified work schedules can vary from one or two hours a day to however many hours are appropriate.

- Job restructuring: Exchanging a few job tasks with another employee or modifying how something is done can make a big difference.

- Modifying the workstation: An example would be providing modified keyboards and lowered file cabinets for a worker who uses a wheelchair.

For example, Lisa works at a restaurant during nonpeak hours so she doesn't have to work so fast. Will, who assembles pizza boxes, works in a separate room so he isn't exposed to the chaos and noise in the kitchen. It's hard for me to visualize Susie working at a grocery store, but in reality, she could—with a job coach and appropriate accommodations. She could work in the early morning, when there are few shoppers and therefore less distractions and noise. She could shelve cereal boxes, because for whatever reason she can read all the names of common cereals as well as the company logos. She might be able to learn how to shelve other items, and if a grocery store were to agree that she could begin by shelving only cereal, they might hire her for several hours a week.

Different Work Settings

The settings in which people with developmental disabilities work vary from supported employment in the mainstream, to protected work situations in the community such as enclaves and mobile work crews, to sheltered workshop settings either in the community or in separate facilities. There are also community experience programs, either volunteer or paid, that meet in various sites in the community. Some states also provide separate work activity centers where adults with severe developmental disabilities can learn daily living skills and some prevocational skills.

As you read the following sections describing various work situations, visualize your son or daughter in each situation, then answer the questions beneath each. The goal is to consider each situation in light of his or her needs, preferences, and interests to help you decide what sorts of work situations or activities might be most appropriate.

Nonwork Day Activity Centers

In nonwork day activity centers, participants usually spend the entire day at a particular facility run by a community agency. The participants in these centers are generally adults with more severe developmental disabilities. They receive training in basic life skills as well as skills to enhance their employability. The activities are highly structured, and there is often a one-to-one ratio of staff to participants to provide enough support for the participants to be fully involved. Ideally, the goal of this sort of program is to prepare participants for some level of employment. Often, and inappropriately, participants stay in these programs for years.

Would your son or daughter like to be involved in a situation such as this?
Yes   No

Is it appropriate for him or her?   Yes   No

Is there an appropriate level of support?   Yes   No

What are the pros and cons of this situation for your son or daughter?

Pros   **Cons**

_____   _____

_____   _____

_____   _____

_____   _____

_____   _____

Community Experience Programs

Susie works in a community experience program called PACE (People Accessing Community Experiences). It meets six hours a day, four days a week. Most community-based programs like PACE try to combine paid employment with volunteer work to round out their day. For a while, the PACE group had a contract to fold newspapers, stuff them in plastic bags, and deliver them. This was paid employment.

Currently, they are largely involved in volunteer activities. They do something different every day at different sites around the county. They clean the pews of two churches and help set up chairs for big events. At another church, they assemble gift boxes for survivors of natural disasters.

Additionally, Susie's PACE program has a rented space in a county building that also houses the county library and the sheriff's department. Here they sort bags of donated clothing they gather from several drop points and prepare them to be distributed to needy people. Susie and her fellow PACE members are picked up at their residences and transported to the different sites. When they arrive, they have juice and coffee and discuss what they'll be doing that day.

In another PACE program, workers make greeting cards, which they sell for a dollar for a box of five cards. This project was conceived and developed by their site manager, Dorothy, who buys the supplies (colored paper, rubber stamps, crimpers, paper cutters, and glue) and teaches them the tasks. She also designs the cards. This has been such a successful work project that the group earned enough money to take a trip to Disney World last year, and they're planning to visit Hershey, Pennsylvania, this year.

Would your son or daughter like to work in a program like this?   Yes   No

Is it appropriate for him or her?   Yes   No

Is there an appropriate level of support?   Yes   No

What are the pros and cons of this situation for your son or daughter?

Pros   **Cons**

_____   _____

_____   _____

_____   _____

_____   _____

_____   _____

Sheltered Workshops

Maria works in a sheltered workshop doing light assembly work for different companies. The workshop crew has put together travel packs for a large pharmacy chain and assembled small parts for appliances. Her sheltered workshop is one of three on the grounds of her residential facility. Each workshop employs six to eight people, including two or three people with developmental disabilities who come in from nearby communities. There is a loading dock and a storage facility to enable the assembled items to be packaged and shipped easily. People with disabilities work in these areas also.

People who work in sheltered workshops are often paid a legally deviated wage that's less than the minimum wage and reflects the slower pace at which the workers do their jobs. Alternatively, they may be paid by the piece or the number of units they complete. Maria walks to her workshop from her apartment on the grounds, and she goes back to her apartment for lunch.

Sheltered workshops, which are self-contained units often in agency settings, have little or no access by the general public and are run by community agencies for the express purpose of employing people who need a more tranquil and protected environment. The people who work in these settings are protected from the noise, chaos, and distractions so often present in workplaces in the community. Additionally, each can work at his or her own pace. The goal is to move these people out into a community setting when they're deemed able to handle it.

When looking for a work situation for their daughter, Maria's parents also visited a large, noisy workshop that employed about forty to fifty people working in one large room at different jobs. Although most of the people were able to work under these circumstances, Maria's parents thought it would be too chaotic for their daughter.

In many states, sheltered workshops are being phased out because they're considered too segregated, meaning that the workers have little or no interaction with the community at large. An answer to this might be to move these workshops into community settings such as places of business or meeting rooms in shopping malls. There are far too many adults with developmental disabilities without any work at all to eliminate any work option as yet.

Would your son or daughter like to work in a situation such as this?   Yes   No

Is it appropriate for him or her?   Yes   No

Is there an appropriate level of support?   Yes   No

What are the pros and cons of this situation for your son or daughter?

Pros   **Cons**

_____   _____

_____   _____

_____   _____

_____   _____

_____   _____

Enclaves and Mobile Work Crews

Enclaves and mobile work crews are similar in that both involve small groups of people with disabilities working in community settings. Both usually consist of four to eight adults with developmental disabilities and one supervisor or site manager from a provider agency. The setting for an enclave is usually a room at a place of business where people with disabilities can work in a relatively calm atmosphere on one or two jobs at a time. Mobile work crews travel from one business to another, performing basic tasks such as house and office cleaning and grounds maintenance. Because they're out in the community, enclaves and mobile work crews provide opportunities for workers to interact with the general public.

Fred, whom you met in chapter 6, works with three other people with developmental disabilities in an enclave at Mitsubishi, where they're supervised by a site manager from a provider agency. They work there twice a week for a total of six hours, but in other enclaves people may work twenty hours a week or more. Their main job is packaging small parts for distribution to auto dealerships. Fred and his coworkers are paid by the piece, which entails a waiver of the minimum wage law.

Fred clocks in and out like everyone else. He makes his lunch in the morning and takes it to work, where he and his coworkers eat in the cafeteria with the other employees. Transportation to and from work is provided by the community agency. Sometimes workers from other parts of the plant drop in during their break to say hello. Fred enjoys his friend Joe, who often comes by at the end of the day to walk out with Fred.

Henry, whom you also met in chapter 6, is a member of a mobile work crew that goes from job to job in the community. They work a total of twenty-five hours a week, cleaning offices and mowing lawns at office buildings. His crew is made up of four or five other adults with developmental disabilities and is supervised by a site manager.

Would your son or daughter like to work in an enclave?　　Yes　　No

Is an enclave appropriate for him or her?　　Yes　　No

Would an enclave provide an appropriate level of support?　　Yes　　No

What are the pros and cons of an enclave for your son or daughter?

Pros	Cons
_____	_____
_____	_____
_____	_____
_____	_____
_____	_____

Would your son or daughter like to work as part of a mobile crew?　　Yes　　No

Is it appropriate for him or her?　　Yes　　No

Is there an appropriate level of support?　　Yes　　No

What are the pros and cons of a mobile work crew for your son or daughter?

Pros   **Cons**

_____   _____

_____   _____

_____   _____

_____   _____

_____   _____

Supported Employment

Lisa works twenty-two hours a week as a dishwasher at Guernsey's Dairy Restaurant in Northville, Michigan. It's a hard job and she often gets hot and sweaty, but she's up to the task. She's always on time or even early, and she's only out sick one or two days a year. Needless to say, she's a valued employee, and she, in turn, loves her job. Recently, on a trip to California with her father, Lisa insisted on wearing her Guernsey's jacket, saying "I want to tell all the people to eat at Guernsey's."

A local provider agency located the job for Lisa, and the owners of Guernsey's were very receptive to employing someone with disabilities. The agency's case manager arranged for a job coach who worked on the job with Lisa for two weeks, helping train her. The job coach still checks in with Lisa from time to time, but Lisa scarcely needs her. The only problem Lisa had was early on, when her boss tried to correct her. Lisa was crushed and afraid she would lose her job. The job coach assured her that this was not the case and spoke to Lisa's boss, who subsequently went out of his way to tell Lisa what a valuable employee she was. The few times Lisa did need correction, her boss was careful to tell her what a good worker she was at the same time.

Lisa, who started at the usual entry-level pay, has received two raises since she began. She's been invited to two of her coworkers' weddings, and recently she was invited to spend the weekend at the home of an older female coworker.

Most people working in supported employment are paid at least minimum wage for the work they do. They can generally work as fast and as accurately as their nondisabled coworkers, although they often work during nonpeak hours so that speed isn't as critical. Sometimes their jobs are modified somewhat to accommodate their needs. They work in regular work sites and are often the only employee with a disability. This gives them the opportunity to socialize and interact with nondisabled coworkers and the general public, as Lisa does.

It's important to note that even people with more severe disabilities may be involved in supported employment in the community, given the appropriate level of support. Chuck, a young man with autism and severe intellectual disabilities, works three hours a week at a university office building. With his job coach's guidance and support, he collects materials from recycling bins and replaces the bins' plastic liners. He's been doing this for six years.

Would your son or daughter like to work in a supported employment situation? Yes   No

Is it appropriate for him or her?   Yes   No

Is there an appropriate level of support?   Yes   No

What are the pros and cons of this situation for your son or daughter?

Pros   **Cons**

_____   _____

_____   _____

_____   _____

_____   _____

_____   _____

Other Work Opportunities

CJ, who cleans houses with his mother, arrives at each house with a big smile of greeting and the latest sports statistics. He and his mother carry in their housecleaning equipment, confer for a moment, and immediately set to work. CJ knows the routine cold. First he collects all the garbage and wastepaper from around the house. Then he goes upstairs to the bedrooms, takes the sheets off the beds and puts them in the laundry basket, and picks up anything on the floor and puts it where it belongs. Then he gets his trusty vacuum cleaner and vacuums the upstairs while his mother works in the kitchen. He works doggedly, stopping only briefly to share another tidbit of sports information. His mother pays him the going wage.

Many adults with developmental disabilities work in a family business, where their parents can dovetail the job to the person's interests and ability. Clyde, for example, works in his father's landscaping business, and Sam works with his father in construction. Maya sometimes works in her mother's office doing clerical tasks even though her mother doesn't own the business. Maya's mother asked her supervisor for permission to bring her daughter to work. Although Maya doesn't get paid by the business, she's getting valuable work experience, and her mother gives her five or ten dollars from time to time so she'll feel compensated for her efforts.

Betty works on the village farm, as do all the villagers, although that isn't her favorite job. She prefers weaving, and she's become quite talented at it and sells the placemats and scarves she makes in the village store. She also volunteers one day a week in a day care center in a nearby town.

Errol works at a supermarket as a bagger. Bert works at a video store shelving returned videos, a job his mother found for him. Our local drugstore recently hired a young man with autism as a cashier. He's a whiz with the cash register and is beginning to interact, if only briefly, with the customers. Others with developmental disabilities can be found working in hospitals, libraries, nursing homes, fast-food restaurants, greenhouses, and many other places too numerous to mention. We are discovering that those with developmental disabilities can do an amazing number of things we never dreamed possible if given the support and training they need.

As you work through the following exercise, bear in mind that it's always best to choose the least restrictive work environment in order to keep your child involved and stimulated. A nonsegregated work environment is preferable to a segregated one if your son or daughter can tolerate it. This will give him or her the opportunity to be more involved in the community and to meet new and interesting people.

FIGURING OUT WHAT YOUR SON OR DAUGHTER WOULD LIKE TO DO

Which work setting would be appropriate for your son or daughter? Check all that apply:

_____ Nonwork day activity center

_____ Community experience program

_____ Sheltered workshop

_____ Enclave

_____ Mobile work crew

_____ Supported employment

_____ Other: _____

_____ Other: _____

In addition to asking your son or daughter what he or she would like to do, review the person-centered plan you generated in chapter 5 so that you'll have his or her likes, dislikes, interests, needs, and abilities uppermost in your mind. Use this information to try to determine where or in what sort of situation he or she would like to work.

What are the things he or she likes to do? _____

_____

What does he or she want to learn? _____

_____

What kind of support does he or she need in order to do the things he or she wants to do? _____

_____

_____

Where, specifically, do you think your son or daughter would like to work? Use the list below to get started on brainstorming some answers with your son or daughter, then figure out what specific type of job he or she would like to have. Check off each type of business your son or daughter might be interested in, then fill in tasks he or she could do in the space provided. For example, if a supermarket seems appealing, perhaps your son or daughter could shelve food items or sweep the floor.

_____ Supermarket or store: _____

_____ Restaurant: _____

_____ Landscaping: _____

_____ Greenhouse: _____

_____ Pet store: _____

_____ Construction: _____

_____ Light assembly (parts, kits): _____

_____ Parent's place of work: _____

_____ Parent's business: _____

_____ Church: _____

_____ Child care center: _____

_____ Hospital: _____

_____ Library: _____

_____ Nursing home: _____

_____ Paper route: _____

_____ Recycling station: _____

_____ Other: _____

_____ Other: _____

Now, using the work settings you've chosen, make a chart on a separate sheet of paper for each. Create four columns with the headings Where, Type of Work, Accommodations Needed, and Support Needed. To fill in the third column, ask yourself what kind of job modifications would enable your son or daughter to work successfully at each job on the chart, and fill in that information. Here's an example with the first three columns filled in:

Where	Type of Work	Accommodations Needed
Supermarket	*Shelving food items*	*Can only shelve cereal and easily recognizable fresh fruits and vegetables*
		Needs to work in the early morning, when there's less distraction
		Another employee will need to bring the loaded cart in from the storeroom

Now ask yourself what type of support would enable your son or daughter to be successful in each of the work settings in your chart. The following list will help you think of the areas in which your son or daughter needs some support:

- Using public transportation

- Grooming and dressing appropriately

- Communicating with other workers

- Managing anger and frustration

- Following rules and routines

- Learning specific job skills

- Protecting himself or herself from exploitation

- Asking for help

- Responding appropriately to feedback

- Completing tasks in the time allotted

- Sticking with tasks until they're finished

- Maintaining quality

- Being willing to learn new things

- ■ Following health and safety rules

- ■ Using tools, appliances, or technology

- ■ Reading signs

- ■ Other: _____

- ■ Other: _____

- ■ Other: _____

Now use that information to fill in the fourth column in the chart. Here's an example:

Where	Type of Work	Accommodations Needed	Support Needed
Nursing home	*Dusting and vacuuming*	*Can't work near small, breakable objects*	*Someone to plug in and unplug vacuum cleaner*
		Needs to work in the early morning or late afternoon, before or after his other job	*Needs training and gentle reminders not to vacuum around people who are talking or napping*
			Needs training and gentle reminders not to talk to residents unless they speak first

These charts should give you a good idea of the types of jobs your son or daughter will enjoy and succeed in, given the needed accommodations and supports.

Find Out What's Available

Contact your community or provider agency to find out what work or volunteer situations are available for your child in the area where he or she lives. If your child decides that he or she would like to have a job, do this as soon as possible, since there are usually waiting lists for the available jobs. These agencies are continually developing job opportunities for their clients, and they will actively look for a job for your child. They can tell you what is available, where, and when.

Your child might choose to take a less interesting or temporary job until a better option becomes available. For example, Lisa worked at a golf course running errands from May through October until her dream job at Guernsey's came through. Alternatively, your child might choose to volunteer in the community until a job becomes available. But, as with living situations, if no jobs are available or none really fit, create your own options.

Create Your Own Options

Most jobs for adults with developmental disabilities are found through a family's personal connections. As mentioned above, many of these adults work in family businesses. Other opportunities are found through friends, extended family, colleagues, or owners of businesses the family patronizes regularly. However, before you pursue these options or create a job for your son or daughter, it's important that he or she be found eligible for employment support by the community agency that will supply funding for employment support services.

Once your child is found eligible for employment support, seek out potential job opportunities for him or her (Condon et al. 2004)—perhaps at a favorite neighborhood store, where he or she might stock merchandise, or perhaps at your place of work, where he or she might collect wastepaper or recycling. If you know a business owner who has a child with a developmental disability, ask that person if he or she would be willing to give your child a job on a trial basis. You could, of course, approach any business owner, but one who shares your perspective or has some connection to your family is more apt to hire your child. It will help if you explain the types of support services your child can get to help his or her performance on the job. Speak to the owner of the business or someone in upper-level management. These people are generally more flexible because they're the ones who determine policy. You can bring your son or daughter with you.

Ask to observe the work environment, and as you do, consider these sorts of questions: Is it noisy and chaotic? Do the other workers seem friendly? Is this the kind of environment your child would work well in? Also be on the lookout for jobs or parts of jobs your son or daughter could master, with support. Point these out to the owner or manager. Sometimes the owner or manager will also have suggestions about what jobs your child could try.

If the owner or manager seems amenable to hiring your child, tell him or her that you'll contact the community agency that funds employment services and that they'll need to contract with a provider agency to send a job coach to begin the job development process. Ask them to send someone to the place of business right away to get the process going. Also find out what type of support services are available for your child and when these services can begin.

Optionally, consider creating a self-employment situation for your son or daughter. For example, he or she could start a greeting card business, mow lawns, or take care of people's pets when they go on vacation. Aaron, a young man with severe multiple disabilities whom you met in chapter 4, loves horses and makes and sells homemade horse treats with the help of his personal assistant. She also helps him make flyers and posts them in his neighborhood and on the Internet to promote his business.

If social action is your cup of tea, join a business association or the chamber of commerce. By participating in these organizations, you can inform potential employers of the need for jobs for people with developmental disabilities. You can also educate them about how supported employment helps assure successful job performance.

The Importance of Being Involved in Meaningful Activities

Work is only part of the picture for an adult with developmental disabilities. Other community activities also bring opportunities to learn, develop friendships, and be productive. Recreation and leisure activities provide fun and relaxation.

If your child is only working a few hours a week or isn't working at all, recreation and leisure activities will be an especially important part of his or her life. Since so many of our sons and daughters don't have jobs, and since, in many areas, jobs for people with developmental disabilities are hard to come by, nonwork activities can play a similar role, providing focus and satisfaction in their lives.

Volunteer activities often bring the same feelings of pride that paid work does while also providing an avenue to social activities and friendships. Churches, hospitals, libraries, the Salvation Army, nursing homes, animal shelters, neighborhood associations, and political campaigns all welcome volunteers. Aaron's personal assistant, who is very creative, helped him develop a volunteer opportunity at the Kalamazoo Nature Center. Although he cannot talk, Aaron volunteers as a docent, showing groups of children around the nature center. His personal assistant records small messages on a communication device, and Aaron activates the device to deliver messages at appropriate times as the group moves about the center. His personal assistant guides his wheelchair.

Volunteer activities can also lead to paid employment. Experience gained while volunteering can help convince a prospective employer of your child's qualifications for a job.

Educational and recreational activities can also lend some structure to the day and provide opportunities to socialize. These types of activities include Special Olympics, church-sponsored programs, and programs developed by parents specifically for people with disabilities. Adult education programs and community recreation programs for the general public are also good options.

Hobbies can bring the adult with developmental disabilities pleasure, recognition, and feelings of competence. For example, Curtis plays the drums at parties. Lisa crochets scarves and baby blankets for her friends and family. Mark and Fred play the chimes in a bell choir every week.

Meaningful Activities for Adults with Developmental Disabilities

Most communities have a variety of activities your child can participate in. Activities and courses offered to the general public by community recreation and education programs are one good option. Also look for programs offered by churches and philanthropic groups that are designed for people with disabilities, as well as specialized camps and Special Olympics. Or there may be day activity programs parents have started in your community.

Community Recreation and Education Activities

Publicly funded community activities must, by law, be made accessible to people with disabilities. Sometimes this means that people with disabilities participate in activities alongside their nondisabled peers. Other times it means that special or adapted programs are created for these people; this is generally done for those with more severe disabilities. Various activities offered through parks and recreation programs and adult education programs may be of interest to adults with developmental disabilities, such as cooking classes, arts and crafts workshops, learning to play a musical instrument, dance classes, exercise programs, and swimming. Field trips and social gatherings specifically for people with disabilities, such as a movie and pizza, are also possibilities.

Activities designed especially for people with disabilities usually have plenty of staff to help everyone participate fully. For activities designed for the general public, your son or daughter may have to bring his or her own support staff, or you may have to help.

Call your community recreation agency and ask them to send you a brochure or list of all their programs. Ask if they have programs and activities for people with disabilities. If they don't, remind them that the Americans with Disabilities Act requires that programs offered by community agencies to the general public must be accessible to people with disabilities.

Programs Sponsored by Churches and Fraternal Organizations

In many areas of the country, churches sponsor activities for adults with developmental disabilities. For example, the Christian Reformed Church in Ann Arbor sponsors a weekly Friendship Fellowship for people with disabilities, welcoming people of all faiths. In Arlington, Virginia, the Young Life Capernaum Partnership provides social opportunities along with gospel to adolescents and young adults. Yachad, the National Jewish Council for the Disabled, sponsors travel experiences for adults with disabilities as well as social groups in various states throughout the country. These activities usually have volunteer staff along with one or two paid staff to assist participants.

Fraternal organizations such as Kiwanis or Alhambra often sponsor get-togethers or outings for people with disabilities. The members of these organizations volunteer to serve as support staff.

Camping Experiences

Some nonprofit agencies provide summer camps and other similar opportunities for adults with disabilities. Susie and Maria attend Camp Fowler in Michigan on occasional weekends throughout the year. It's a typical camp experience with bonfires, marshmallow roasts, hayrides, arts and crafts, and lots of sing-alongs. Needless to say, they love it. Camp Fowler has weeklong sessions during the summer, including one for children and adults dependent on respirators. They even have a tree house that's accessible by wheelchairs. Camps for adults with developmental disabilities are located across the United States, and most of them employ well-trained staff. Call state or local parent organizations for people with developmental disabilities to help you locate camps in or near your state.

Special Olympics

Special Olympics provides year-round training and competition in summer and winter sports for children and adults with intellectual disabilities. Adults with severe and multiple disabilities are included, and people of all ability levels are welcomed.

These athletes are grouped with others of similar ability levels in training and competition. There are accredited Special Olympics programs throughout the United States and in many other countries.

Special Olympics provides a wide variety of sports programs to people who would not normally have access to them. I will never forget watching Lexi compete in the broad jump. She walked slowly and carefully to the line and jumped—about five inches. She turned happily to her parents in the audience and, with great pride, gave them a thumbs-up. Everyone cheered.

Participating in Special Olympics can enhance physical fitness and motor skills while also providing opportunities to socialize. And, most importantly, it provides a sense of pride in a job well done. The organization employs a combination of paid and volunteer staff with experience and training in working with people with disabilities.

Parent-Initiated Activities

In Ann Arbor, informal groups of parents have developed such activities as the Just Us Club, a drop-in activity center for adults with disabilities that includes exercise, bingo and other games, crafts, music, dance, and parties; and Common Chords, a handbell choir for adults with disabilities and their nondisabled friends. Parents often volunteer to staff these activities, sometimes with the assistance of paid staff. These types of activities usually aren't listed in your telephone directory, and they can be a bit difficult to track down. The best way to find out about them is to contact your local parent organization.

Take some time to think about what recreational activities your son or daughter would like to participate in. Also ask your son or daughter about this, and review the person-centered plan you generated in chapter 5.

What recreational activities are a good fit for your son's or daughter's interests, abilities, and likes and dislikes? _____

_____

_____

What kinds of supports would your son or daughter need to participate in these activities? _____

_____

_____

Remember, having a job is an important part of being an adult. Besides the financial benefit, work can give your child feelings of pride and accomplishment he or she may not experience anywhere else. If your son or daughter is lonely or isolated, work will also provide important opportunities to socialize and interact with others.

Involvement in meaningful activities also brings feelings of pride and accomplishment. Participating in community activities also provides welcome opportunities to socialize and interact with others. Keeping busy and active can make an important contribution to your child's quality of life.

Next Steps

Most adults with developmental disabilities need a combination of work and other activities to fill up their day. Locating employment opportunities and other meaningful activities for your child may be relatively easy, or it may be difficult, depending on the community and your child's interests and abilities. Whatever the case may be, it's important to keep trying until you find some fulfilling activities that are a good fit for your child. The effort is well worth the rewards it will bring your child.

The last important component of a good place to live is the professional caregiving staff. The next chapter will help you understand what traits make a person a good caregiver and help you locate and hire the best professional caregivers for your child.

CHAPTER 8

Finding Good Caregivers

Now that you're well on your way to finding your adult child a good place to live with opportunities to be busy and productive, it's time to take a look at the last major piece of the puzzle: professional caregivers. Once your child moves out of your home, these are the people who will provide the types of support he or she needs to live a full, rich life.

We want our sons and daughters to live in an atmosphere of respect and affection, cared for by people who understand them and want the best for them. After all, this is what we've provided for them at home. We want no less for them when we can no longer take care of them.

Is it possible to find people who can provide this type of care? Yes. Is it easy to find these people? No, it isn't easy, but it can be done. There are many amazing people out there who are committed to caring for adults with developmental disabilities. These professional caregivers often provide services above and beyond the call of duty, and for minimal pay. For example, during the tragic flood in New Orleans in 2005, many professional caregivers stayed with their charges for hours or days and helped them escape the floodwaters.

Our fervent wish is that our sons and daughters live with someone who loves them, and that's why we think of family first. But having a family member as caregiver may not be feasible or even desirable. Fortunately, most long-term professional caregivers do come to love the people they care for and think of them as family. In fact, these caregivers often become like members of our own families as well.

Perhaps you've read stories in the newspaper about abusive, irresponsible caregivers who leave their charges alone for long periods of time or even hit them. There are irresponsible caregivers, of course, but hopefully this chapter will help you steer clear of them. It will also help you figure out what qualities you and your child are seeking in a professional caregiver and give you some guidelines for locating and hiring caregivers who fit your requirements.

Professional Caregivers

Professional caregivers, known as direct care workers, direct care professionals, or personal assistants, come from all walks of life. Some are students working their way through college. Some are young people without experience or training in this field who, initially, are just looking for a job that pays a little more than minimum wage. Others feel that they're doing God's work by becoming a direct care worker. Still others have a person with a disability in their family and want to use their experience and understanding to help other families.

Many professional caregivers are single mothers, and some come from broken homes. Others have left dead-end factory jobs in search of work where they can make a difference. People come into caregiving for a variety of reasons, but those who stay do so because they feel that they're improving the lives of the people they care for.

Many professional caregivers are so dedicated that they voluntarily work overtime, without compensation, to ensure the well-being of someone they work with. For example, Kathy is very kind and loving and often stays longer than her shift requires in order to provide continuity and support if the person she's caring for is having difficulty. Peggy, who does a lot of needlework at home, taught Lisa how to crochet (and continues to help her undo her mistakes). A direct care worker taught Maria how to play the recorder.

Many direct care workers go beyond what anyone expects of them. One manager of a group home went out of her way to locate a family who would be willing to invite one of the women she takes care of to their home for Thanksgiving and Christmas. The parents of the young woman lived too far away to visit her, and she was often lonely when the other residents got together with their families. At Our Lady of Providence Center, several direct care workers invited residents without families to their homes for weekends and holidays. Other professional caregivers have even adopted young people with developmental disabilities who didn't have any family of their own.

Most of these dedicated professional caregivers believe in the inner potential of the people they care for, regardless of what psychologists or doctors say. They share a deep commitment to the people they work with and support. To give you a better idea of the range of people who do this sort of work and their qualities, let's take a closer look at two direct care workers, Penny and Bill.

Penny

Penny started working as a professional caregiver in an intermediate care facility for teenagers when she was eighteen years old. She had been working as a cook in a residence for elderly people, but she wanted to be more directly involved with people. She had done a lot of babysitting when she was growing up, and she really liked kids and taking care of them. So even though it involved a pay cut, she applied for a job at the intermediate care facility.

They almost didn't hire her because they thought she was too shy and would have difficulty taking charge of eight teenagers at a time. She may have been shy with other adults, but she wasn't shy with the teenagers in her care. They loved her, and she loved them. She says that she treated them the way she herself wanted to be treated.

She worked the midnight shift and went to Eastern Michigan University in the mornings. She slept in the afternoons after school and did her homework during the night when the residents were sleeping. She got her degree, thought briefly about graduate school, and then decided she wanted to continue being a direct care worker. Soon she was hired by a local community agency to work as a live-in house manager for three young men who lived in a house in the community.

Penny, who has been a direct care worker for over twenty years now, is a warm, funny, outgoing woman. These days she works with, supports, and encourages a variety of young adults with developmental disabilities, including my daughter Susie. (She's provided us with respite care for many years.) She recently married a coworker she met at the teen facility many years ago. He works as a teacher's aide in the special education department of the local school district.

Penny says that what she likes most about being a direct care worker is watching people grow and become able to do things they couldn't do before. She says that the most important traits of a direct care worker are patience, empathy, humor, and compassion, traits she herself has in abundance.

Bill

Bill has been a direct care worker for the past fifteen years. After graduating from high school, he worked in retail management for four years but found the job less than inspiring. He wanted to find a job where he could give something back, so he started working with sixteen- and seventeen-year-old boys with developmental disabilities at a church facility to which his family occasionally made donations.

Bill, who grew up in a single-parent household, had been a troubled teen. Now that he was twenty-two, he felt he could understand these teens with developmental disabilities. He felt he had something to offer them: he could help redirect them and help them make good choices, as he was trying to do in his own life.

Bill describes a day that made it all worthwhile. "I'd been trying to help Frank learn to tie his shoes on and off for about nine months, and we had gotten stuck on the last step where you tie the two loops together. And then one day he did it! It was the high point of my life—and still is, for that matter. At that moment, I knew I had chosen the right job for myself. To me these guys are normal. I think of them as part of my family. Probably most good caregivers feel that way."

Today Bill is the program director at the facility he started working at fifteen years ago. He handles licensing, staffing, and resident care issues. When asked what he looks for in a direct care worker, he says, "I'm looking for a 'mom' kind of person, preferably someone who has children of his or her own. Someone who is patient, mature, and has a sense of humor and a certain humility. I don't care very much about experience or education." He adds, "The people you care for become part of your family if you're the right person for the job."

Parents as Caregivers

As parents of adults with developmental disabilities, we often don't think of ourselves as caregivers, but we are. We didn't choose to be caregivers, as Penny and Bill did, nor are we paid for the care we provide. But when we think of finding a professional caregiver for our children with developmental disabilities, we often think of what we ourselves provide and want to find someone who can do the things we do.

I usually don't think about the ways I provide support for Susie because they've become second nature to me. When Susie is with me, I brush her teeth twice a day because she has limited range of motion in her wrists and hands and can't reach all areas of her mouth. She's in charge of bathing herself, but I wash her hair every other day to make sure it's clean and completely rinsed of shampoo. Several times a day I check to make sure her face is clean, something she's not good at since she hasn't mastered the art of looking in the mirror to monitor how she looks.

Although Susie picks out her own clothes and dresses herself, I need to check that her pants aren't on backwards, for example. I need to remind her to put on a heavy coat when it's cold outside and not to wear a heavy coat when it's warm because she has difficulty understanding or remembering this. She can make a good approximation of a peanut butter and jelly sandwich, but otherwise I prepare all of her food. (However, I often let her choose the menu.) I need to cut up her meat because she sometimes chokes on large pieces.

As I give my caregiving duties some thought, I could go on and on: I take Susie shopping for food and clothes. I take her to all community activities. I make all her appointments, and I accompany her to the doctor and dentist, often translating for both Susie and the doctor. I invite her friends over for dinner—often at her suggestion. I play games with her when I'm not too tired. I try to calm her when she gets upset, using the bag of tricks I've developed over the years. And, of course, I try to anticipate her wants and needs. I expect Susie's professional caregivers to do all these things.

Describe the caregiving duties you perform for your son or daughter. Be specific.

_____

_____

_____

_____

_____

_____

_____

_____

_____

Add to this list from time to time and try to make it as complete as possible. You'll be able to use this list when you talk to potential direct care workers about job requirements and your son's or daughter's wants, needs, and preferences.

Your Strengths and Weaknesses as a Caregiver

You have many, many years of experience as your son's or daughter's caregiver, and you've learned a great deal about caregiving even though you may not realize it. Like everyone else, including professional caregivers, you have both strengths and weaknesses when it comes to caregiving. Take some time to think about your strengths and weaknesses, then describe them below.

What makes you a good caregiver for your son or daughter? _____

_____

_____

_____

_____

_____

What are some things you wish you did better as a caregiver for your son or daughter? _____

_____

_____

_____

Hopefully, you accept the fact that you aren't perfect! Professional caregivers aren't perfect either. What makes a good caregiver is an abundance of strengths to counterbalance the inevitable weaknesses that all human beings have. Remember this anytime you feel inadequate, and definitely keep it in mind when looking for a direct care worker for your child.

The support provided by a professional caregiver is wide-ranging and should include most everything you've done for your son or daughter through the years—and more. The goal of a professional caregiver is to help your child function as independently as possible while providing the support he or she needs to live a satisfying life.

Different Strokes for Different Folks

Since every adult with developmental disabilities is a unique human being, each will need a different set of supports from direct care workers. Some adults with developmental disabilities need support services twenty-four hours a day, seven days a week, every day of the year. This means that three direct care workers, each working an eight-hour shift, are needed to cover the twenty-four hours. Some people with developmental disabilities need awake staff at night when they themselves are asleep. These people are usually medically fragile or have epilepsy that isn't completely controlled. Other adults need support only during waking hours, and still others need only occasional support in order to keep their lives running smoothly.

Depending on the type and intensity of support needed, direct care workers take on a variety of roles. They can function as teachers, modeling and demonstrating new ways of doing things; as helpers or prompters for tasks that are already known but not quite accomplished successfully; as cheerleaders for effort and progress toward a goal; as interpreters, helping their charges communicate their feelings and preferences and helping them understand the world around them; as mediators in misunderstandings and disputes; and, above all, as problem solvers, smoothing over difficulties or preventing them from occurring in the first place. Some direct care workers provide total physical care, feeding, bathing, and dressing the person with whatever help the person can muster. Others serve to keep their charges safe and protect them from danger. A good direct care worker is flexible, understands what needs to be done, and finds a way to do it.

To help you see the range of possibilities, let's take a closer look at some of the adults you've met in this book and the kinds of support their direct care workers provide. However, keep in mind that your child's needs will be unique to him or her and that the person-centered plan can provide guidance about the level and types of support he or she needs.

Jean

Jean, who has mild cognitive disabilities and is fairly self-sufficient, sees her direct care worker twice a week. She helps Jean with such things as paying bills, shopping for clothes, and arranging for visits to her aunt who lives out of town. Her direct care worker also arranges for several of the adults she supports to meet once a week for dinner and socialization, something she's initiated on her own that goes beyond her paid duties. Jean also has a case manager, a social worker who monitors her needs and situation once a month.

Fred

Fred, who has mild to moderate cognitive disabilities, including autism, has a direct care worker seven days a week for sixteen hours a day plus a sleep-in worker at night. He shares his caregivers with his two housemates. Fred has good self-care skills and largely needs his direct care workers for guidance and supervision. Recently, he proudly announced to one of his direct care workers that he had ordered a pizza with a coupon he received in the mail. She received this information with a certain degree of shock and wasn't quite sure how to respond. On the one hand, she was proud of Fred for his accomplishment (and he was proud of himself). On the other hand, it became clear that Fred didn't realize he had to pay for the pizza. This is a good example of why people like Fred need a direct care worker during all of their waking hours.

Scott

Scott, who has severe cerebral palsy and moderate cognitive disabilities, needs one-on-one support many times during the day for such things as dressing and bathing. He also needs his diapers changed and condom catheter emptied several times a day. He shares his direct care workers with one other resident in his house. He and his housemates also need awake staff at night to monitor their medical needs. His direct care workers have to be able to interpret the single syllables Scott uses for words and his subtle cues, such as a glance or a hint of a smile, in order to understand what he wants or needs.

Maria

Maria is legally blind and has mild cognitive disabilities as well as autism. Her self-care skills are good, so she needs little help in this regard. She's also good at following routines and begins and ends her days with routines she's practiced for many years. However, she can't solve new problems or cope well with new situations, so she needs full-time caregivers to provide guidance as the need arises. She shares her direct care workers with six to eight other women, who all require a relatively minimal amount of support. She also needs help with socializing and protection from danger and exploitation. Maria's direct care workers encourage her to join in on activities to prevent her from retreating into her own world. They also encourage her to speak up for herself if something's bothering her, since she tends to be very passive.

Mark

Mark's direct care worker provides support for Mark and his housemate for an hour each morning and an hour or two each evening. She helps the men get started on their day in the morning, and in the evening she helps them plan and prepare for the next day. She also helps them shop and drives them to evening activities.

The Duties of Direct Care Workers

The direct care worker's duties are largely driven by the person-centered plan and, if employed by an agency, agency requirements. The person-centered plan provides the direct care worker with information about the strengths, interests, needs, and goals of the person they're working with. Agency and licensing requirements ensure that workers are qualified to dispense medication, understand and respect recipient rights (the rights of the adult with developmental disabilities to public services and supports), have first-aid training, and are familiar with SSI and Medicaid requirements. In addition, you can provide the direct care worker with a list of supports you feel are important for your child's well-being.

This means that, among other things, the direct care worker's duties can include any of the following:

- Brushing teeth if the person can't do it alone, or checking to see that the job is done correctly.

- Making sure that the person is clean. This includes helping him or her learn how to wipe after using the toilet, or changing diapers if needed.

- Cutting up food as needed, or reminding the person to cut and chew carefully.

- Providing transportation to work, appointments, and community activities, or training the person to use public transportation unaccompanied.

- Accompanying the person as he or she shops for food and clothing and providing appropriate assistance.

- Making sure the residence is clean and safe, and practicing fire, flood, and tornado drills.

- Monitoring health, including giving medication as needed, making sure that medication is under lock and key if necessary, and making medical appointments.

- Filling out paperwork required by community agencies, Social Security, Medicaid, licensing agencies, and so on.

Most direct care workers provide support for more than one person and sometimes up to eight adults. Yet they also have to individualize all activities and assistance based on each person's interests, strengths, and needs. This is time-consuming and requires a lot of patience and forethought. In many situations where the direct care worker is responsible for more than one adult, another direct care worker is on call to help individualize activities; for example, the second worker might be called in if the group wants to go out but one person is sick and needs to stay at home.

Part of the direct care worker's job is interacting with parents and families, involving them in making decisions and asking them for suggestions on how to best help and support the person with developmental disabilities. Some direct care workers are good with parents, others not so good. Often these workers interact very well with adults with developmental disabilities but are shy or uncomfortable with parents and other family members. If this is the case for you, be sure to weigh the good job the worker is doing with your child against any less-than-perfect interactions with you.

Providing a Caring and Supportive Environment

Above all, direct care workers must provide a supportive and caring atmosphere for the adults under their care. Although this often isn't specifically listed as a duty when a direct care worker is hired, it is essential to the well-being of an adult with developmental disabilities.

A supportive and caring environment can be difficult to describe and measure. It includes many of the things mentioned in chapter 4 as ways of enhancing the quality of life of adults with developmental disabilities. It also means that the living environment isn't driven by rules, such as going to bed at a certain time or having to eat everything that's put in front of you. Rather, it should be informed by individual preferences while also keeping in mind what's needed for health and safety. Here are some ways a direct care worker fosters a supportive environment:

- Listening attentively and taking the time to understand what the person wants to communicate.

- Giving the person choices about what to do, when, and with whom and respecting those choices, whether or not the caregiver agrees with them. However, a good caregiver will take the time to explain the different options and the pros and cons of each.

- Treating the person as an adult.

- Having positive yet reasonable expectations for change and growth without constantly trying to "fix" the person.

- Providing structure and predictability while also helping the person understand and prepare for changes in routine.

- Easing the transition from one activity to another.

- Understanding that "bad" behavior is a way a nonverbal person communicates "no" or "I don't want to" or "I don't like that" and changing the environment, requirements, rules, or activities instead of blaming the person for this behavior.

- Creating a family atmosphere by encouraging a sense of belonging among group members, taking pride in everyone's accomplishments, insisting on zero tolerance for teasing and put-downs, and promoting respect among roommates and housemates.

- Keeping the person active and involved by planning activities in which the person can experience success.

- Providing the right amount of support—neither too much nor too little.

- Acting as an advocate when necessary, explaining to others the needs and wants of the person with developmental disabilities.

Responding to Parent Suggestions

As a parent, you play a key role in the development of your child's person-centered plan, which guides agencies and caregivers working with your son or daughter. However, you can also play a direct role in setting out the duties of your child's direct care workers. You can provide additional information about how to interact with your child and some background information on why he or she might behave in a certain way.

Susie occasionally has temper tantrums in which she yells, stamps her feet, and sometimes hits herself. This can be very distressing, especially for people who don't know her as well as I do, because it's often difficult for them to figure out the cause or calm her down. To help with this, I asked for a meeting with Susie's social worker and direct care staff. I hoped that if they could understand what might be causing her problems, they could prevent the problems from occurring or calm her down sooner. I explained that her temper tantrums usually occur when she isn't allowed to do something she wants to do; because of her limited speech, she often can't explain what she wants or why, so she ends up feeling frustrated and helpless. I also pointed out that her problems are sometimes caused by general anxiety or physical distress, such as premenstrual tension or constipation. I told them that my experience had been that, in most cases, in order to prevent or allay her anxiety, what Susie needed was more explanation and more time to understand a situation and what it requires of her.

One of the direct care workers said that she had found that offering Susie a distraction, such as taking a message to the office or taking a bath, could also help her take her mind off her anxiety. This reminded me to tell them that Susie likes to listen to music, and that this too can help soothe her. I also suggested to the staff that, beyond the usual rewards of a hug or a thank-you, Susie be given some particular responsibility, such as setting the table, carrying someone's bags, or pushing the cart in the grocery store. Susie loves to be helpful, and being in a position to help others makes her very proud—and takes her mind off her anxiety.

Many parents write out instructions for direct care workers, particularly if their child is more severely disabled and can't express himself or herself verbally. Two parents I know, one with a son with severe cognitive disabilities and the other with a son with severe physical disabilities, have written notebooks for their sons' caregivers. These include such things as a list of favorite foods and favorite activities, what might cause him to get upset and how to calm him if he does get upset, and extensive suggestions and directions to help caregivers understand where he's coming from and how to develop a supportive environment for him. One mother said that she reminds all new staff that people sitting in wheelchairs all day tend to get cold and that her son needs to be dressed more warmly than a person who's more active.

What are some of the most important instructions and suggestions (other than information that appears in the person-centered plan) that you'd want to give to a new caregiver working with your son or daughter? Be specific. _____

_____

_____

_____

_____

_____

_____

_____

_____

Modify this list from time to time as your child's likes, dislikes, needs, and interests change. Give a copy of this list, or more detailed notes if you have them, to any new caregiver to help him or her understand your child. A list of instructions and suggestions should also be appended to your long-range plan. This kind of list can ensure that whoever takes care of your child when you're not around will understand the best ways of interacting with him or her.

As direct care workers really get to know your son or daughter, they'll develop their own procedures and responses. These will incorporate many of your suggestions, but they'll also include some new ways of working with and relating to your child. Even though you have your own tried-and-true repertoire of strategies, a direct care worker's new perspective can often suggest ways of doing things that are equally effective or even more effective.

Try not to micromanage every little detail of the interactions between direct care workers and your child. Remember that these caregivers are professionals, often with valuable training and experience. Allowing direct care workers to use their creativity in providing support to your child will demonstrate that you respect them and help you maintain a good working relationship with them. It will also ensure a better outcome for your child.

Creating a Good Work Environment for Direct Care Workers

Caregiving brings many of its own rewards, which is good, since direct care workers are usually paid very poorly. The earnings of many are below the poverty line. They often have limited health benefits or no health benefits at all—or any other standard job benefits, for that matter. They often work nights and weekends and frequently have split shifts. But playing a role in the growth, progress, and general happiness of an adult with developmental disabilities can bring caregivers a sense of pride and satisfaction. On the other hand, giving of themselves as they do, direct care workers often suffer from stress or burnout.

Parents can help make direct care workers' jobs easier by providing as supportive a work environment for them as possible. Recognition of the hard work they do can show that you respect them and their work, and respect can go a long way toward making up for poor wages. Thanking them for going the extra mile can also help caregivers feel that their work is appreciated. You can help assure them that you think they're competent by following their advice. And, of course, supplementing their wages in some way can make their job more tenable.

Also try to make a personal connection at whatever level seems appropriate. Remember that they are people with lives and families of their own. Specific ways to do this include giving them gifts occasionally, remembering their birthdays, asking after their families, inviting them to dinner, bringing other members of your family to meet them, or writing thank-you notes telling them how well you think your son or daughter is doing (assuming this is the case). Creating a good work environment for the people who are caring for your child will go a long way toward compensating for the lack of esteem a poor salary implies. You can also help in more concrete, hands-on ways, such as by buying needed supplies, volunteering to help with cleaning, leading a group of residents in arts and crafts or other activities, and so on. This type of involvement demonstrates your own commitment to making the environment enjoyable for all.

Even though they may not intend to, parents often appear to be criticizing direct care workers. In their zeal to make everything perfect for their son or daughter, these parents become very picky about what meets their approval. This can be very discouraging for direct care workers. Be aware that these caregivers need as much encouragement as you can provide to keep them functioning well in a very demanding job.

Community Agencies

Once your child is deemed eligible for services from a community agency, that agency plus Medicaid will pay direct care workers' salaries and benefits in addition to providing services. They may pay caregivers directly, or they may do so through a provider agency or by giving you or your child the money to pay the direct care workers. These arrangements are worked out between you and the community agency.

Provider Agencies

Often the funding and staffing functions are divided between two agencies. Provider agencies are private nonprofit agencies that hire and train direct care workers and job coaches. (You'll learn more about the types of agencies in chapter 9.) Generally, community agencies will proved the funding and give you a list of provider agencies from which you can choose. There are two advantages to hiring staff from a provider agency rather than doing your own hiring: the agencies provide up-to-date training, and they provide backup staff when scheduled workers must be absent for any reason. In addition, they require that staff never leave a client without support, even if it means staying beyond the hours of their shift.

Since you'll usually have a choice among several provider agencies, take the time to interview the director of each agency and figure out which is best. You'll want to ask questions along these lines:

- What is the agency philosophy?

- What kind of training do direct care workers receive?

- How many clients does the agency serve?

- What is the ratio of clients to staff?

- In situations where there is only one direct care worker, what will happen if, for example, one client wants to stay home and another wants to go to the movies?

You can also ask to meet with others who have a family member receiving services from that particular agency to ask them how they feel about the agency and its staff.

Accreditation agencies such as CARF (Commission on Accreditation of Rehabilitation Facilities) provide oversight of these agencies and ensure that they provide quality services to their clients. ANCOR (American Network of Community Options and Resources) has developed a set of principles and standards of conduct for provider agencies and direct care workers. The National Alliance for Direct Support Professionals can provide Web based training to direct support workers.

Formal Requirements for Direct Care Workers

Most agencies have specific requirements when hiring direct care workers. These include an application process that asks for past experience (both work and volunteer), references, and education, plus an interview. Agencies usually require that the applicant have a high school diploma or equivalent. Good references are a must. Applicants must also have a valid driver's license and proof of insurance.

Before actually hiring a direct care worker, agencies conduct a criminal background check (with either their statewide system or a private agency that does these background checks) and check the applicant's driving record. Applicants are also required to have a recent physical examination and tuberculosis and hepatitis tests, at their own expense, in order to be employed.

Many agencies require applicants to have first-aid training before they're hired, while others require that direct care workers complete this training within a few weeks after being hired. Most agencies run training programs for their direct care workers to update their knowledge and skills regarding working with adults with disabilities.

The required interview process is oriented toward determining applicants' commitment to working with people with disabilities and ensuring they have an understanding of the responsibilities of a direct care worker. To that end, they're usually asked questions along these lines:

- Why do you want a job as a direct care worker?

- Do you have any personal experience with children or adults with disabilities?

- Have you worked as a caregiver for senior citizens or children?

- Do you think of yourself as a problem solver? Please explain.

- What do you think you'll be required to do as a direct care worker?

The interviewer might also ask how long the applicant worked at any previous jobs and why the applicant left those jobs. This might provide evidence of how responsible the applicant is.

When an agency is hiring a direct care worker for your child, you and your son or daughter can be part of the hiring process. You can ask to screen applications, participate in interviews, and be involved in the final hiring decision. If you choose to hire a direct care worker yourself, you can follow the same process as a community agency.

What Most Parents Want in a Direct Care Worker

I recently asked some parents what they were looking for in a professional caregiver. The first things most of them said had to do with commitment and dedication. "An inner calling" said one parent, and "Not just a job" said another. Of course, parents were also looking for professional caregivers who were responsible and would show up on time every day.

Direct care workers, like Penny and Bill, echo the same sentiments. A sense of commitment and certain personality traits seem more important than education, training, or experience. This is because caregiving, unlike most other jobs, requires the involvement of the whole person, not just a set of specific skills.

Here are some other personality traits parents frequently identify as being important:

- Patience

- Sense of humor

- Empathy

- Good problem-solving abilities

- Compassion

- Willingness to try new ways of doing things

- Ability to be kind yet firm

- Common sense

These traits often aren't mentioned in the job requirements, and it can be difficult to find out if a candidate for a caregiving job has these traits during a standard interview. However, if you ask the applicant to spend some time interacting with your child as part of the application process, you can get a better feel for these sorts of qualities. You and your child may also get a sense of whether the applicant will prove to be a good match for him or her.

What are some things you're looking for in a professional caregiver for your son or daughter? Be sure to ask your son or daughter, too. Be specific. _____

_____

_____

_____

Monitoring Direct Care Workers

Once a direct care worker is hired, you can't just sit back and relax. You need to monitor the direct care worker from time to time, and more often at first, to ensure that he or she is the right kind of person for your child. First of all, ask your child directly about his or her opinion of the direct care workers. Also ask your child what he or she has been doing recently to find out if the caregivers are encouraging him or her to be active and involved.

You can monitor the situation formally by scheduling monthly meetings with direct care workers to discuss how your child is doing. You can also monitor a new caregiver informally by dropping in a few times to visit your child. When you do this, ask yourself these kinds of questions:

- Does my child seem happy?

- Does he or she seem to like the caregiver?

- Is he or she clean and neatly dressed?

- Does my child seem willing to go back to his or her residence after an outing with me?

- Is the residence clean?

- Is the TV on whenever I visit? Are they watching too much TV?

- Does my son or daughter seem to be getting along with his or her housemates?

- Does my child have any unexplained bruises?

When you're visiting, ask the direct care worker what your son or daughter likes to do and who seems to be his or her closest friend. These questions should give you an idea of how well the worker knows your child. Putting all of the information you've gleaned together should give you a picture of how well the direct care worker interacts with your child and whether the worker is providing good support for him or her.

Monitoring your child's direct care workers as well as his or her living situation as a whole is an ongoing job. This is something your other adult children or other family members should take over when you're no longer able to do it. It would be good to go ahead and identify which family members might take on this task and to involve them in your own monitoring from time to time so that they'll become familiar with the process and with the details of your son's or daughter's situation.

When a Direct Care Worker Doesn't Work Out

Sometimes you may find yourself unhappy with a direct care worker. You may feel that a certain caregiver doesn't work well with your child, or you may feel that he or she is neglecting your child or treating him or her badly.

First of all, sit down with the person and tell him or her how you feel. Provide good examples to back up your criticism. If the direct care worker can't or won't change, call the service-provider agency and tell the director how you feel. The director of the agency might arrange a meeting with you and other families the worker is serving to discuss the matter, or the director might act unilaterally and either transfer or fire the worker.

If you've hired the direct care worker yourself, be sure to document your criticisms and give the person fair warning. If things don't change, fire the worker. Don't feel guilty if you have to do this—remember, your child's happiness and well-being is at stake.

Next Steps

The major components of a good life for your child are a good place to live, opportunities to be busy and productive, and good people to take care of him or her. The next chapter will provide you with suggestions on how to interact with community agency staff to create the best situation for your child and get the support services he or she needs. Then, chapter 10 will help you put together everything you've learned to create a plan that will make this life possible for your child.

CHAPTER 9

Working with Community Agencies

There are many reasons why a large majority of parents aren't in contact with the community agencies that provide services and supports to adults with developmental disabilities. Many parents simply aren't aware of the existence of these agencies and that adults with developmental disabilities have legal rights to services and support. Parents who do know about these agencies often have assumptions about them based on out-of-date information regarding their policies and procedures. These parents don't realize that, these days, services and supports are developed individually to fit each person's needs, interests, and preferences and that the adult with a disability and his or her parents are actively involved in determining these services and supports.

Other parents prefer to have their son or daughter live at home with them. They feel that their son or daughter doesn't need services from a community agency and that they can provide for their adult child with developmental disabilities better than any agency can. Others families feel that they aren't ready to commit to anything, or they don't know what they want or what to ask for. Therefore they don't see any reason to contact a community agency.

Still other parents have had unfortunate interactions with community agencies in the past and want nothing further to do with these agencies, or they may just be generally suspicious of community agencies. In the past, these agencies might have alienated parents by suggesting institutionalization for their son or daughter (McCallion and Kolomer 2003).

If you haven't been in contact with community agencies in regard to your son or daughter, hopefully what you've learned in this book has convinced you to consider making contact now. This chapter will help clarify which agencies provide which sorts of services. It will also help you work more effectively with agency staff to develop appropriate supports and services for your child, both now and in the future. You'll also learn techniques for resolving any conflicts that arise while working with community agencies.

Reasons to Contact Community Agencies

Whether you feel that your child needs some services now or that he or she will need them in the future, it's important to contact the appropriate community agency to establish your child's eligibility for services and find out what services are available. These agencies provide a wide range of services, including respite care, housing, work and work-related activities, direct care workers, job coaches, personal assistants, health care and mental health care, transportation to and from activities and appointments, and case management services. You can also find out about personal assistance for your child to help him or her get dressed, brush his teeth, and bathe, and homemaker services can help you or your son or daughter with cooking, shopping, and cleaning. Community agencies can also help you with home modifications (like ramps and railings) and adaptive equipment to help your child function more easily and make your life easier.

Your child can utilize some of these services now, even if he or she is living at home with you. This is especially true of work and work-related services for your child and respite services for you. If you still feel hesitant, keep in mind that some of these services can enhance your child's life immensely by enabling him or her to live a busy and productive life, whether in your home or in the community.

Take some time to consider what type of services and supports would benefit your son or daughter and your family, both at this point in time and in the future. You might refer back to the person-centered plan to make sure you've covered all the bases.

Supports and services that would be helpful at this point in time: _____

_____

_____

Supports and services that would be helpful in the future: _____

_____

_____

Agencies Have Changed

About twenty years ago, I was called by a staff member of a community agency who said that they had an opening in a group home for Susie. They told me I had twenty-four hours to decide whether or not to take it. In those days, I was working and taking care of Susie, so twenty-four hours didn't give me enough time to see the place, much less make a decision. I had to turn the offer down, and I never got another call from that agency.

Recently, the successor to that agency contacted me with an offer to move Susie from her church-run facility into a group home in the community. I was given over a month to make a decision. During that time, the community agency arranged for me to visit the group home, meet the staff, and talk to other residents' parents. I also met with the community and provider agencies to discuss the situation. Although I ultimately turned this offer down, my relationship with the community agency never faltered. Our annual meeting to update Susie's service plan took place a few months later, and it was one of the best meetings we ever had.

Agencies have changed. Their policies have changed. People with disabilities are no longer viewed in terms of what they cannot do; rather, the main purpose of community agencies is to provide the supports necessary to help adults with disabilities function as well as they can in whatever environment they're in.

Community agencies can't place adults with disabilities against their will or the will of their parents. Parents and the adults themselves can refuse inappropriate or undesirable placements without fear of rejection or retribution. Agencies generally allow adequate time for all involved to make informed decisions about new living situations, and the living situations are better too, being more attractive and homelike.

Various state and federal laws mandate that people with disabilities be given choices about where they live and work, that they are to be aided in participating in community activities as much as possible, and that family support be provided as needed. The terms currently in use to describe this orientation are "self-determination" for the person with disabilities and "parent empowerment" for the person's family.

The principle of self-determination, which is used to guide decisions affecting the person with developmental disabilities, essentially means that all decisions affecting that individual are based on his or her own preferences. The adult with developmental disabilities, with the help of family members, chooses what activities (both work and recreational) to be involved in, where to live, and who his or her direct care workers will be (within certain agency parameters).

Parent empowerment means that parent and family involvement is also mandated—in developing programs and supports and in making decisions. Family members can activate an appeals process anytime they feel their wishes aren't being heard or acted on. Armed with these rights, you and your son or daughter should generally feel satisfied with your interactions with community agencies and the service plans that result.

Many parents believe that working with an agency means having to share their innermost thoughts and feelings with agency staff. This is not true. Your privacy, and that of your child, must be respected. Beyond the information needed to develop an appropriate service plan, you need not share anything about your family you don't feel comfortable sharing.

Locating the Right Agency

Throughout this book, I've used the generic term "community agency" when referring to the agencies that provide services, supports, and funding to adults with developmental disabilities because each state uses different names for the many agencies providing these services and funding. There are even variations within the state at the county or local level. Each agency has its own criteria for eligibility, yet only through the cooperation of several agencies can a good service plan be developed.

In its 2004 report, the President's Committee for People with Intellectual Disabilities stated that "there are so many different programs administered by so many different agencies that people with intellectual disabilities and their families face a maze of overregulated, fragmented, sometimes conflicting, and always complex systems of benefits and supports" (President's Committee for People with Intellectual Disabilities 2004). The good news is that any community agency you contact can usually refer you to the agency that provides funding for specific services and supports you're seeking. A good case manager at any given agency is in touch with other agencies and can help you access and coordinate the services and supports your child needs.

One of the simpler ways of locating an appropriate community agency is to ask other parents the name of the agency that provides services to their son or daughter. Or you can contact your state or local chapter of the Arc or United Cerebral Palsy, to name just two organizations run by consumers (people with disabilities and their families). You can find these in the business white pages of your telephone book, usually listed under your state or county name, or on the Internet (see the Resources section for a helpful list of national Web sites). These consumer-based organizations can give you the name and phone number of the community agency that provides the type of services you're seeking.

Consumer or parents' organizations are also good sources of information about your child's legal rights, sources of funding, and how each community agency functions. Being in contact with these organizations can be immensely helpful in other ways, too, by helping you to feel less alone, connecting you with support groups, and allowing you to access the wealth of experience and information other parents in your situation have to offer.

Record the names and phone numbers of any helpful consumer or parent organizations here or somewhere you can easily find them.

_____

_____

_____

Another way to begin your search for community agencies is to look in the state, county, or city government pages of your telephone book. Or you can begin on the

Internet by typing www.(*the name of your state*).gov. This will help you access your state government and its many departments, such as the Department of Labor and the Department of Education. You should look for a department with one of the following names: Department of Mental Health, Developmental Disability Services, Department of Health and Mental Hygiene, Department of Human Services, or something similar. Under each department you'll find lists of community agencies and services. You can call any of these departments or agencies to find out which state agency is responsible for providing services to adults with developmental disabilities. You can ask these state agencies for the name of the local community agencies you should contact.

On the county or city level, you'll find agencies with names like Community Services Agency, Community Mental Health Agency, Human Services Agency, Social Service Agency, Community Health Agency, and so on. These agency names will often be preceded by the name of the city, county, or regional center (when two or more counties are included in the same agency).

You'll need to explain to whatever agency you contact that you're looking for supports and services for your adult child with developmental disabilities. Ask the agency who they serve and what kind of services and supports they provide. Once you've tracked down the appropriate agencies, record their names and phone numbers here or somewhere you can easily find them. Also list the services each provides.

_____

_____

_____

Types of Agencies

There are two main types of agencies that provide funding for adults with developmental disabilities. The first is the Social Security Administration, a branch of the federal government, which provides these adults with basic funding for the necessities of life. Specific types of funding available include Supplemental Security Income (SSI), Social Security Disability Insurance (SSDI), Medicaid, and Medicare.

Only low-income people are eligible to receive SSI, but most adults with developmental disabilities fit that category because their parents' income isn't counted. You can go to your local Social Security office to arrange for SSI payments for your son. SSI pays for basic sustenance: primarily food, clothing, and shelter.

Those who are eligible for SSI are usually eligible for Medicaid and food stamps, too. Medicaid and food stamps are accessed through whatever community agency provides subsidies to low-income people. Besides paying for medical care, Medicaid also provides funds for personal assistants or direct care workers. The Food Stamp

Program provides funding for the purchase of certain foods. Your local community agency can probably help you arrange for Medicaid services and food stamps for your son or daughter.

In order for your child to receive SSDI and Medicare, he or she must be the child of a retired or deceased worker, or he or she must have worked for a certain period of time before becoming disabled. There are no income restrictions on this money. Like SSI, SSDI pays for food, clothing, and shelter. Many people eligible for SSDI and Medicare are eligible for Medicaid as well because their income is low. Your local Social Security office will help you sort out whether your son is eligible for SSDI or SSI.

The second type of funding agency pays for services, such as developing individualized service plans, providing direct care workers, case management, and referral. Although these community agencies are supposed to provide services for all who are eligible, they often can't due to insufficient funding by the federal government. (These agencies also receive funding from state and local government.) These agencies generally have priority systems for the delivery of services to adults with disabilities.

Another type of agency consists of private, nonprofit providers who act as employment agencies, supplying the staff needed for service delivery. Community agencies contract with and provide funds to the provider agency. Providers hire and train direct care workers, job coaches, site managers, and other workers to carry out the service plans. The State Vocational Rehabilitation Services Agency, a line item in the federal Developmental Disabilities Act, also provides funding for job training and job-related services. This agency has local branches; see the state government pages in your local phone book.

Other Sources of Funding

Some public and private agencies provide grants and other subsidies to people with disabilities if funding is available. These are not entitlements, as SSI and SSDI are. There's usually a waiting list for this type of funding. For example, the U.S. Department of Housing and Urban Development (HUD) provides rent subsidies for low-income people. Known as Section 8 rent supports, these can be accessed through your local housing commission or community agency. Fannie Mae works with lenders to ensure that mortgage funds are available to people from all walks of life. This organization is committed to diversity and can help you obtain a loan with no down payment and low interest rates, options that might make it more affordable to purchase a home for your son. The USDA's Rural Housing Service provides home loans in rural, nonfarm areas for people with disabilities, and the Home Repair Loan and Grant Program can provide funds for making a home accessible to someone with disabilities. This type of funding can usually be accessed through a bank or lending institution that offers mortgages.

Many private faith-based organizations provide housing for adults with developmental disabilities at no cost to the person or his or her family beyond the person's SSI or SSDI. And, finally, if you're sixty-five or older and caring for an adult child with disabilities, your local affiliate of the Council on Aging may be able to provide funding for respite care.

What are the names and phone numbers of your local community agencies that provide supports and services to people with developmental disabilities? What services, supports, or funding does each agency provide? How is eligibility determined?

_____

_____

_____

_____

_____

Special Needs Trusts

SSI, SSDI, and Medicaid are supposed to provide for the basic needs of adults with developmental disabilities. However, you may want to set up a special needs trust, also known as an amenities trust or supplemental needs trust, to provide your son or daughter with the extras that may make his or her life more enjoyable. Special needs trusts can provide for extras such as furniture, personal items, and travel. In some instances, a special needs trust can be used to purchase a home; in this case, the trust would own the home and your son or daughter would pay rent to the trust.

You don't have to be wealthy to set up a special needs trust for your son or daughter. The amount of money you set aside in the trust can be just enough to buy a new TV or DVD player occasionally or to pay for a yearly visit to an out-of-state family member. Since the amenities the special needs trust can pay for are limited by law, the trust needn't be overly large. The trust can be set up to begin providing funds right away or at the time of your death.

It's important to set up a special needs trust so it doesn't jeopardize your child's governmental benefits (SSI, SSDI, and Medicaid). If you decide to set up such a trust, be sure to use an attorney well versed in the rules and regulations governing special needs trusts. Local parent organizations may be able to give you referrals to attorneys experienced in this field. An excellent resource on guardianship and special needs trusts is *A Family Handbook on Future Planning*, by Sharon Davis, Ph.D. (2003). It can be downloaded from the Arc Web site.

What Happens After You Contact an Agency

If you're requesting services or funding for your adult child, the agency will first determine his or her eligibility for supports and services. You and your child will be required to fill out an application that details your child's developmental history as well as his or her current diagnosis. An important part of this intake process will be face-to-face interviews with you and your child.

The agency staff will ask you for copies of any assessments your child has had. They may ask you for medical reports, school reports, reports from previous agencies that have provided funding or services to your child, and so on. They will also probably do some assessment themselves. Findings of eligibility can take several months.

Since many of these community agencies are underfunded, they tend to first provide services to those adults with more severe disabilities, those whose living situations are very precarious, and those in need of emergency services. Those with elderly or chronically ill parents are also given a high priority.

If your child is found eligible for services according to agency guidelines, the agency will provide a case manager to coordinate whatever services he or she needs. The case manager will also contact any other community agencies that can provide services to your son or daughter or help you contact them.

The next step is usually a person-centered planning meeting to determine your child's strengths, interests, and needs and to develop an individualized plan of services and supports. The plan will be monitored by the agency and revised yearly. (You can monitor it too.) Once the agency has agreed to fund services and supports, they'll help you contact provider agencies who will provide the direct care staff needed to deliver the services. You and your child should be fully involved in all of these steps. If you're dissatisfied with any part of these procedures or the resulting decisions, there's an appeals procedure available to you.

Preparing Yourself for the First Meeting

It's important to know as much as possible about an agency before meeting with its staff. It's also important for you to know as much as possible about your child's needs, preferences, and interests so you can help him or her communicate these to the agency or describe them yourself if need be.

Gather Information About Your Son or Daughter

The person-centered plan you created in chapter 5 is an excellent way to communicate information about your child to the agency. Since your child will participate in the meeting, be sure that you've discussed the purpose of the meeting with him or her and the topics that might be addressed. When you go to the meeting, bring along any assessments of your child that were completed within the last three years or so: psychological or medical evaluations and any reports written by people who have worked with your child. Ask the agency what other information they require.

Gather Information About the Agency

When you first contact the agency, ask them to send you a descriptive brochure, or visit the agency and pick up whatever handouts they have. Keep a record of the name and telephone number of each agency you contact and the name of staff members you talk to. You might also consult with other parents whose adult children receive services from each agency under consideration.

Recently, when I considering moving Susie from Michigan to California to be near one of her brothers, I contacted a nationwide parent organization to ask them if there was a parent I could talk to who lived in California who could give me information about the California system of services and supports. I had already made an appointment with the regional agency serving the area in which my son lived, but I felt I needed to hear from someone whose son or daughter was receiving services from that particular regional center. The parent who contacted me was extremely helpful in explaining the California service-delivery system. What she shared, coupled with information I received from the regional center, gave me a much more complete idea of what I could expect if Susie were to move to California.

Understand the Agency's Philosophy

Federal and state laws require that people with developmental disabilities be integrated into the community as much as possible. This laudable goal means that most community agencies will first recommend a living situation in the community in which your son or daughter would share a home with no more than one or two other adults with disabilities. It also means that many agencies prefer to place adults with developmental disabilities in supported employment in the community rather than in sheltered workshops or day activity centers, which these agencies consider segregated. However, this is not necessarily a good model for all adults with developmental disabilities. Research (Bouras and Holt 2003) and anecdotal evidence attest to the fact that often these adults become understimulated and isolated in one- or two-person settings. If the person prefers to live in a group setting, he or she should be allowed to do so. Other options do exist in most communities, but you may have to ask about them.

Also, although most states have closed their large-scale institutions and have stopped placing adults with developmental disabilities in nursing homes, some states still do. Many states are pushing to close intermediate care facilities also. Find out where your state and local agencies stand on this issue before beginning to plan with them. If, for whatever reason, you aren't happy with the residential options an agency suggests, your local parent organization can generally inform you about residential situations that aren't on the agency radar. These residential situations may be faith-based, privately funded, or larger than the agency prefers.

Making the Most of Meetings

Write a list of your questions, concerns, and preferences before going to any meeting with agency staff. (This is a list for your personal use, so it need not be well written.) It's a good idea to do this over a period of several days before the meeting to ensure that you get everything down. Refer to your list during the meeting to be sure all of your questions and concerns are addressed. During the meeting, take time to make notes of the answers the agency gives you. It can be hard to retain everything you learn, especially at the beginning when you're taking in a lot of new information. Taking notes and asking questions at the meeting will help. Also remember that you can call your child's case manager in the future to ask for clarification if you need to.

At the first meeting, the agency should make its philosophy, policies, procedures, and criteria for eligibility clear. If not, don't hesitate to ask them to do so. They should also give you written information regarding your adult child's rights and a description of the appeals process you can utilize if you disagree with any decisions made, including your child's eligibility for services.

At the end of the meeting, be sure you write down all decisions that have been made and what the agency has promised to do. Be sure you're clear on the next steps: exactly what the agency will do and what you need to do. If possible, go ahead and set a date for the next meeting.

Dealing with Nervousness

Many parents feel nervous when they go to meetings about their son or daughter because they see these meetings as being essential for their son's or daughter's well-being. While these meetings are important, realize that you're involved in a long-term, step-by-step process. No single meeting will make or break your child's future, and even if things do take a wrong turn, you always have the appeals process to turn to.

Another cause of nervousness is not knowing what to expect. Be sure to ask your contact person or case manager what the meeting will cover, so you can prepare yourself. This may mean gathering additional information about your son or daughter or bringing an advocate with you who knows the laws and can help you plead your case.

You may feel nervous because you fear you'll become too emotional during the meeting. First, realize that your situation is difficult, and that it's okay to feel emotional about it from time to time. It assuredly wouldn't be the first time (or the last) that a parent was overcome with emotion at an agency meeting. It may help if you bring a trusted family member or friend with you to every meeting. That will lend some normalcy to the situation and may keep you more even-keeled. Plus, you'll feel that you have someone in the room who loves you and supports you. A surreptitious hand squeeze or pat on the knee can go a long way toward helping relieve your tension. This person can also help you clarify what is being said, help you express your feelings and opinions, and afterward may be able to remind you of anything about the meeting you've forgotten.

You can prevent a great deal of nervousness if you inform yourself about how the agency functions and understand your child's legal and human rights—and your own. In addition, learning and practicing assertiveness and negotiation skills can help you get your opinions and preferences across.

Understand Your Legal Rights

To get a general idea of your adult child's legal rights and your own, contact your state protection and advocacy service (P&A). The Protection and Advocacy System was set up by the federal Developmental Disabilities Act for the express purpose of protecting the legal rights of people with developmental disabilities and their families. P&A deals with housing, employment, and SSI issues, to name but a few. In addition to giving you legal information and advice, your P&A can provide you with an advocate if you need one. Local or state parent organizations can also be very helpful in clarifying your legal rights, and they, too, can often provide you with an advocate if you feel the need for one.

Although you'll need to consult with others to understand all of the details of your child's legal rights, there are a few basic and important rights to keep in mind: If an agency finds your child eligible for services, he or she has the legal right to receive those services and supports in a timely manner. Both you and your child have the legal right to be actively involved in decisions regarding the type and level of services and supports he or she will receive. And, finally, you have the right to appeal any decision made by a public agency, and these agencies are required to provide you with information regarding the appeals process. Your state P&A can assist you with an appeal.

Guardianship

Your clout will increase if you are your adult child's guardian. Many parents don't know that after age eighteen (or age twenty-one in some states) adults with developmental disabilities can legally make all of their own decisions. However, most agencies do respect parent involvement no matter what age their son or daughter is. If you think it necessary for you to continue to have legal control over certain aspects of your son's or daughter's life, you must go to court to become his or her guardian.

Adults with developmental disabilities may need a guardian if they have great difficulty giving informed consent for medical procedures and release of information. Guardianship is also helpful if the person has difficulty making decisions related to work and living situations. Full guardianship gives the guardian complete decision-making authority and responsibility for the person. Another option is limited guardianship, which gives the guardian authority and responsibility only in selected areas, such as medical care or where the person lives; this allows the adult with developmental disabilities to make his or her own daily decisions regarding what to wear, what to eat, what to do, and who to do it with, for example.

Guardianship isn't for everyone, but it does give parents legal standing in advocating for their adult child with developmental disabilities. When you go to court to seek guardianship, you must present evidence (usually a current evaluation) as to why your son or daughter needs a guardian. Your child will be represented by a court-appointed attorney to ensure that his or her rights aren't violated. You can name one of your other children or another family member as standby guardian to ensure your son or daughter has a guardian in case you become incapacitated.

Understand Your Human Rights

While it's important to know your own and your child's rights under law, it's equally important to understand that you and your child have basic human rights as well, rights we all share as citizens of this country. Reminding yourself of your human rights can often give you the courage and sense of control to exercise your legal rights. The following human rights pertain to both you and your child in your interactions with community agencies:

- The right to ask for and receive complete explanations from agency staff

- The right to express opinions and be heard with the same respect accorded others

- The right to have procedures followed as outlined in agency guidelines

- The right to have the law followed

- The right to say no or disagree without feeling uncooperative or difficult

- The right to take time to slow down and think

- The right to change your mind

- The right to be free of threats or pressures

Remind yourself of these rights before and during each meeting, and don't hesitate to remind others of your rights if necessary.

Learn and Practice Assertiveness

Assertiveness is the direct and appropriate expression of opinions and feelings while respecting the rights and feelings of others. This includes expressing both agreement and disagreement and both positive and negative feelings. It also includes asking for explanations and standing up for your son's or duaghter's legal rights. Practicing assertiveness in your interactions with agency staff will usually result in productive meetings. Aggression, on the other hand, involves violating others' rights through personal attacks or yelling, which inhibits communication. When interacting with agencies, both aggression and lack of assertiveness generally result in programs and services that are poorly thought out and ineffective.

It may be that you're afraid to voice your opinion or disagree with things an agency proposes. But if you aren't assertive, you may allow others to violate your child's legal and human rights. You can't be shy when you're at meetings about your child. If you're basically a shy person, you'll have to steel yourself to speak out. Keep reminding yourself about how important the decisions made at these meetings are to your child, and remember that you are his or her advocate. Other than your child, you may be the only one at that meeting who has his or her best interests at heart. Agency staff may care about your child, but they're paid by the agency and must follow agency rules.

For example, if an agency staff member were to say to you at your first meeting, "Your child isn't eligible for services," an assertive response would be, "My son must be formally evaluated for eligibility before you can say yes or no." A nonassertive response, on the other hand, might be, "Oh no! I don't know what to do." Nonassertive parents generally accept everything the agency says without question. An aggressive parent might say something like "Damn it! You're screwing me over, and I'm going to sue you," often accompanied by the pounding of tables and slamming of doors.

Here's another example: Suppose an agency staff member were to respond to a request you've made by saying, "We don't do that here." An assertive response might be, "What does the law require you to do? I understand that agencies in other counties provide these services." A nonassertive response might be, "That's too bad," which signals that you accept the situation and will probably result in inappropriate or insufficient services or supports for your child. An aggressive response might be, "What do you mean you don't do that here? You're just saying that because you're trying to save money." In this case the question is aggressive because it's really a disguised attack.

Assertiveness can mean asking for help directly. Saying "Can you help me?" in a firm, clear voice rather than demanding help can result in the staff doing their utmost to help your child get the services and supports he or she needs. Asking for help and saying thank you are two of the most disarming things you can do at a meeting.

If you are assertive, this doesn't mean that agency staff will agree with everything you say and want. Disagreements can and will occur, and they won't always be avoidable or even problematic. Disagreements are a consequence of differing expectations, values, opinions, and constraints. You may expect a type of service that a particular agency isn't required to provide. Or the agency may want to provide a service for your child that he or she doesn't want or that you consider inappropriate. Assertiveness skills can help clarify and solve these types of differences.

Don't fear disagreements. Differences of opinion can be an important element in the planning process (Markel and Greenbaum 1979). They can also result in more creative solutions to problems and better service plans. Therefore, the goal isn't to avoid disagreement at any cost, but to clarify, negotiate, and resolve them whenever possible.

Negotiation

Assertiveness can also entail negotiation, which involves problem solving and compromise. Negotiation ensures the most positive results for each side in the disagreement. In order to negotiate effectively, both sides must be flexible and open to exploring new and creative options. Both sides must also respect and trust each other.

Before embarking on any negotiation, carefully consider your list of questions, concerns, and preferences. Prioritize them from the most important to your child at this time to the least important or those things that can be dealt with at a later date. The most important and immediate concerns should be the focus of your negotiations.

Try to understand where the agency is coming from and prepare yourself to counter these arguments. Is the agency trying to save money? Are they having difficulty hiring enough skilled staff to provide services? Do your child's evaluations show that he or she doesn't require the services?

If the agency is trying to save money, try to think of a cost-effective way they can provide the services to your child. For example, he could share the service with others. If there are no skilled staff who can perform certain services, you can offer to help locate trained staff or provide training to staff yourself so that they can work effectively with your child. If evaluations indicate that your child isn't eligible for certain services and you think he or she is, you can seek other reputable evaluations or you can carefully document the situations in which your child needs those services.

Here's an example of the negotiation process: Lisa is a very capable young woman in many ways, with mild intellectual disabilities and speech impairment. She works part-time as a dishwasher and is aware of many things that are going on in the world. Her local community agency decided that she didn't need any support services at all.

Her father didn't agree, and in advocating for her, he pointed out that Lisa is very vulnerable and will buy practically anything that someone wants to sell to her. She'll open the door to anyone who rings the bell, and she'll talk to virtual strangers about her personal business. In addition, she still can't manage money even after many years of instruction. Her father feels that Lisa can indeed stay home alone without supervision for several hours at a time and certainly doesn't need one-on-one supervision, but she does need to have someone nearby to ensure her safety.

The compromise Lisa's father negotiated with the agency resulted in the agency providing direct services to Lisa two hours a week to help her with managing money and shopping for food and clothing. The agency also agreed that Lisa could live with two other young women who received full-time services so that their staff could watch out for her safety.

It's important that agency decision makers be involved in the negotiation process. That way other staff members won't make promises that the agency can't fulfill. In addition, you can explore solutions that lower-level agency staff might have been unaware of. In Lisa's case, it was necessary for all of the case managers involved to get together and agree and then ask their supervisor for approval before the decision could be finalized.

If you've had negative experiences with agencies in the past, you'll have to put aside those feelings and begin new negotiations with a clean slate. Operate on the assumption that the agency wants to help your child even though their approach may be different from yours. Bear in mind that most community agency staff really care about adults with developmental disabilities and their families and want to help, but often they're limited by insufficient funding and legal constraints.

Key Points

Remember that, ultimately, your son or daughter should be making the decisions. First of all, fully inform him or her about what will be discussed at each meeting. Ask for his or her feelings and preferences on each topic under discussion. Tell your child what your preferences are and ask if he or she agrees. If you and your child disagree, give careful weight to his or her preferences.

If your child can't communicate effectively, you'll have to look at each decision from his or her point of view as well as your own. You can either observe your child's nonverbal responses carefully as you explain things to him or her, or you can think back to situations that can serve to illustrate your child's feelings on similar matters. At meetings with agencies, be sure you communicate your child's feelings and preferences if he or she can't do so.

Take your time when making decisions, and don't let yourself be railroaded. If you feel you need more information, ask for it. You can request that you and your child visit any residential situation under consideration so that you can meet the staff and the other residents.

Don't make decisions out of gratitude or because you don't want to hurt a staff member's feelings. While they may have worked hard to locate the services and options they're suggesting, this is not a reason for you to choose a particular option. You can thank them for all of their hard work and still disagree with what they suggest.

Dare to go with your instincts as to what is best for your child, even if it conflicts with what the agency recommends. Generally, you'll find that disagreement with the agency's recommendations is quite acceptable. This wasn't always the case in the past, but it is now.

Keep the lines of communication open no matter how disappointing any particular meeting is. Take time to regroup your forces and gather new information, then ask for another meeting to discuss the matter. Invite someone who knows your child well to accompany you to the next meeting and speak up on his or her behalf. Even if you've gone through an appeals process and lost, keep talking.

Much progress has been made in the last few years regarding the delivery of services to adults with developmental disabilities, but we still have a ways to go. Join with other parents and parent organizations to lobby on the local, state, and national level for increased funding for services. On the federal level, urge your senators and representatives to increase Medicaid funding so that wages for direct care workers can be increased. On the local level, speak to your county commissioners or city council members about increasing taxes to pay for underfunded services.

Next Steps

Hopefully this chapter has given you a better understanding of the often confusing variety of agencies out there and helped you make a start on researching which are appropriate to provide services and funding to your child. The tips and techniques you've learned here should help you interact with these agencies more effectively, something you'll probably need to do to develop the best possible long-term life plan for your child.

Now that you're armed with this information, along with details on residences, caregivers, and work and other meaningful activities, you're ready to create a long-term life plan for your child. This plan should be designed with your child's preferences, needs, and abilities in mind, which you explored in chapter 5. The final chapter in this book is devoted to helping you create this long-term life plan—an important milestone that will assure your child's future quality of life and also set your mind at ease.

CHAPTER 10

Creating a Plan for the Future

The first part of this chapter will help you collect, in one place, all the information you currently have about your son or daughter. You probably have most of this information on hand but have it scattered all over the place. It's important to gather it all together in one place and to formally document the information you have in your head but have never written down.

If you're well organized, you've probably already set up files with most of the information about your child neatly arranged and easily accessible. If you don't have a file of important papers pertaining to your child, make one now. Go ahead and gather whatever important information and documents you have on hand: your child's birth certificate, Social Security number, person-centered plan from this book, and any service plans from community agencies, for example. (If you don't have a copy of your child's birth certificate, you can order one online by contacting the department of vital statistics in the state or county in which she was born.)

Include any recent medical assessments. It would be a good idea to schedule a physical exam for your child so that his or her medical status will be up to date. At the same time, you can make a copy of your child's immunization record and bring any shots up to date. Also include a copy of your will, any guardianship documentation, and your child's special needs trust, if you've set one up for him or her.

Assembling all this information in one place will take a certain amount of time, but it's well worth the effort. It ensures that if you were to disappear or become incapacitated tomorrow, your child's life wouldn't be turned upside down. No one will have to search frantically to locate the name of your child's doctor or a contact person at a community agency. Your child will still be able to eat his or her favorite foods and participate in his or her favorite activities. You should also write down and include your opinions and any concerns about the current setup so that others will know your preferences for your child's care.

The second part of this chapter will help you set goals and plan for your son or daughter's future. This will take more time, as a lot of thinking and research is involved in planning for the future. Hopefully you've begun this process as you've worked your way through this book. Whether you've already begun to make a long-term plan or you're just getting started now, remember to consider your child's preferences and discuss all important decisions and information with him or her, to the extent possible, and with the rest of your family.

You won't be able to complete either of these sections in just a session or two. There's a lot of information to compile, and gathering some of it will take some time. Plus, thinking about the future can be quite emotional; you should stop for a break if you feel drained or overwhelmed. A break can last a week or even a month, but try not to let it run longer than that. Tell yourself that you need to see this project through to its conclusion, for the sake of your child and for the sake of your family. Reward yourself from time to time if it helps you stay motivated, and remember that completing this task will be the greatest reward. Once you've put together a good life plan for your child, you'll feel that a great weight has been lifted off your shoulders.

CURRENT INFORMATION

Since it's a good idea to update your son's or daughter's current information periodically, make a copy of this form to fill out, so you'll always have a fresh copy available.

Date: _____

Your name: _____

Your address: _____

_____

Name of your son or daughter: _____

Your son's or daughter's address: _____

_____

Your son's or daughter's birthday: _____ Age: _____

Social security number: _____

Diagnosis: _____

_____

Doctors' names, addresses, phone numbers, and specialties:

_____

_____

_____

_____

_____

Immunization record: _____

_____

Dentist's name and address: _____

_____

Therapist's name and address: _____

Medications (include dosage and purpose): _____

_____

_____

_____

_____

Health insurance (Medicaid, Medicare, other) and account or ID numbers: _____

_____

_____

_____

Who to contact in case of emergency (include full names, phone numbers and addresses): _____

_____

_____

_____

Names and phone numbers of respite care workers, sitters, direct care workers, or personal assistants plus how you feel about each of them: _____

_____

_____

_____

_____

_____

Names of agencies that provide services (include contact person and/or case manager, phone numbers, a description of services provided, plus how you feel about each agency): _____

_____

_____

_____

_____

_____

_____

_____

_____

Helpful parent organizations (include contact people and phone numbers and what sort of information or assistance they can provide): _____

_____

_____

_____

_____

Funding sources (SSI, SSDI, rent subsidies, and so forth) and current amount paid:

_____

_____

_____

Bank name, address, and account number (of your son or daughter), if applicable:

_____

_____

Name of guardian and standby guardian (include phone numbers and addresses):

_____

_____

_____

_____

Location of guardianship papers and other important documents: _____

_____

Names and addresses of close family members: _____

_____

_____

_____

_____

_____

Names and addresses of close friends: _____

_____

_____

_____

_____

_____

Description of your son's or daughter's current living situation and pros and cons from both your point of view and his or her point of view: _____

_____

_____

_____

_____

_____

Description of your son's or daughter's current work situation and recreational activities and the pros and cons of each from both your point of view and his or her point of view: _____

_____

_____

_____

_____

_____

Be sure to attach a copy of your son's or daughter's current person-centered plan from chapter 5. If this isn't possible, then attach a separate sheet of paper and list the most important information in each of the following categories:

- Strengths and abilities

- Needs

- Interests and favorite activities

- Favorite foods

- Special routines

- How to calm him or her down

- Any special routines (for example, a bedtime routine)

Plan for the Future

Now that you've finished documenting and gathering all of your adult child's current information, you're almost ready to write out a detailed plan for his or her future. Though this may have seemed a monumental or impossible task when you first started this book, hopefully you now have a good idea of what you and your child want for his or her future.

Writing a Plan for the Future

As you fill out the document below, try to be as specific as you can. But remember that things change—often for the better. Describing the type of situation or option that you and your child have decided on is generally better than just jotting down the name of a residence or place of employment. This way others will be able to understand the reasons you have made certain decisions and can follow through on your wishes if a particular residence closes or changes a great deal. It's also a good idea to revisit your plan from time to time to reflect changes in your child's situation and preferences and the options available to him or her.

You can use the following outline to write a plan for the future. As you use the form below, you may want to provide more details on certain aspects of the plan. Compile them separately and attach them to the plan. If you feel at a loss about any aspect of the plan, review the relevant chapter to remind you of your options (see chapter 6 for living situations, chapter 7 for work and other meaningful activities, and chapter 8 for professional caregivers).

You can also write a more personal letter to your family describing your preferences, hopes, and fears for your child with disabilities. Often called a letter of intent, this is not a legal document; it's merely a recommendation. Although it may accompany your will, it doesn't have the legal status of a will. A letter of intent tells your family what your goals are for your child and how you'd like him or her to live after you're gone, but it allows your family members to make their own decisions as to what they think is best.

Don't hesitate to add anything you think is important to your will or letter of intent. For example, you might note that you want your child to have specific personal items of yours, his or her favorite household items, or specific family photographs. You might want to include a special message of love to your child with disabilities. You might also want to include a special word of thanks to your other children for the understanding and support they've provided to your son or daughter with developmental disabilities.

And finally, and as always, be sure to include your child's preferences in any plan for his or her future. It is your child's life, after all. You should also discuss this plan in depth with your family and particularly with your child's guardian or standby guardian. Make sure everyone fully understands your reasons for choosing certain options and your goals for your son or daughter.

MY PLAN FOR THE FUTURE OF MY ADULT CHILD WITH DEVELOPMENTAL DISABILITIES

Date: _____

My name is _____

This is my plan for _____

I am parent, guardian, brother, sister, other (circle all that apply).

My hopes are _____

_____

_____

_____

My worries and concerns are _____

_____

_____

_____

Residential Situation

I want _____ to live at (location) _____

Why? _____

_____

_____

I want _____ to live near (whom) _____

Why? _____

_____

_____

I think the following living situation is best. Describe in detail.

_____

_____

_____

Why? _____

_____

_____

My second choice is _____

_____

Why? _____

_____

_____

I would like _____ to live with _____

Why? _____

_____

_____

Work and Other Activities

I think the following work situation will work out best: _____

_____

Why? _____

_____

_____

My second choice is _____

_____

Why? _____

_____

_____

_____

I would like _____ to be involved in the following activities: _____

_____

_____

_____

Why? _____

_____

_____

_____

_____

Caregivers

I feel that direct care workers, personal assistants, and other caregivers should have the following qualities: _____

_____

_____

Why? _____

_____

_____

_____

I want everyone to treat _____ with _____

_____

Please monitor the residential situation and direct care workers at least once a month, and more frequently if possible.

Why? _____

_____

_____

_____

When you monitor look for such things as _____

_____

_____

Please be sure that my son's or daughter's daily life is based on his or her preferences and interests. Please remember to involve my son or daughter in any decisions affecting him or her.

In Conclusion

I hope this book has given you and your son or daughter a feeling of optimism about his or her future. You and I have been companions on a long journey. As parents of sons and daughters with developmental disabilities, we've faced many challenges and experienced many joys and sorrows. Even though there have been rough patches, we've done the best we can. The life plan you've created for your child is a testament to your love and care for your child and your commitment to his or her well-being.

Any plan for the future must evolve over time. You may want to change things on occasion, or you may think of some things you want to add. Your child's capabilities, interests, and preferences may change. The options available to him or her and the laws governing them are bound to change, too. Review your child's life plan from time to time and adjust it as needed.

But for now, sit back and take a deep, satisfying breath. You might even have a good cry—of relief and release. You have just taken a giant step, one that many parents are afraid to attempt. You should feel justly proud of yourself.

Resources

Web Sites

Abledata: www.abledata.com (information on assistive technology)

Ablenet: www.ablenet.com (catalog of communication tools and assistive technology)

Administration on Developmental Disabilities: www.acf.hhs.gov/programs/add

American Association on Intellectual and Developmental Disabilities: www.aaidd.org

American Council of the Blind: www.acb.org

Ancor: www.ancor.org (provides training and advocacy for direct care workers)

The Arc: www.thearc.org (advocates for the rights and full participation of adults and children with developmental disabilities)

Association for Persons with Severe Handicaps: www.tash.org

Autism Society of America: www.autism-society.org

Commision on Accreditation of Rehabilitation Agencies: www.carf.org

Epilepsy Foundation: www.efa.org

Little People of America: www.lpaonline.org

Muscular Dystrophy Association: www.mdausa.org

National Alliance for Direct Support Professionals: www.NADSP.org (provides training and credentialling for caregivers)

National Association of the Deaf: www.nad.org

National Council on Aging: www.ncoa.org

National Council on Independent Living: www.ncil.org

National Disability Rights Network: www.protectionandadvocacy.com

National Fragile X Foundation: www.nfxf.org

National Organization for Rare Disorders: www.rarediseases.org

National Rehabilitation Information Center: www.naric.com

Osteogenesis Imperfecta Foundation: www.oif.org

QualityMall: www.qualitymall.org (information about supports and products for people with disabilities)

Social Security Administration: www.ssa.gov (information on Supplemental Security Income and Social Security Disability Insurance)

Special Olympics International: www.specialolympics.org

Spina Bifida Association: www.sbaa.org

United Cerebral Palsy: www.ucp.org

Voice of the Retarded: www.vor.net

Publications

Barclay, J., and J. Cobb. 2001. *Full Life Ahead: A Workbook and Guide to Adult Life for Students and Families of Students with Disabilities.* Montgomery, AL: Southeast Regional Resource Center, Auburn University.

Beach Center on Families and Disability. 1994. *How to Make Positive Changes for Your Family Using Group Action Planning.* Lawrence, KS: University of Kansas.

Cook, A., and S. Hussey. 2002. *Assistive Technologies: Principles and Practice.* St. Louis, MO: Mosby, Inc.

Davis, S., ed. 2003. *A Family Handbook on Future Planning.* Chicago: The Arc of the United States and Rehabilitation Research and Training Center on Aging with Developmental Disabilities, Department of Disability and Human Development, College of Applied Health Sciences, University of Illinois at Chicago.

Etmanski, A. 2000. *A Good Life for You and Your Relative with a Disability.* Vancouver, BC: Planned Lifetime Advocacy Network (PLAN).

Hardman, M., C. Drew, and M. W. Egan. 2002. *Human Exceptionality: Society, School, and Family.* Boston: Allyn and Bacon.

Harries, J., R. Guscia, N. Kirby, T. Nettelbeck, and J. Taplin. 2005. Support needs and adaptive behavior. *Mental Retardation* 110(5):393-404.

Heller, T. 2000. *Aging Family Caregivers: Needs and Policy Concerns.* Family Support Policy Brief 3. Available at www.familysupport-hsri.org/resources/policy_3.html.

Heller, T., J. Caldwell, and A. Factor. 2003. *Supporting Adults with Intellectual and Developmental Disabilities and Their Families in Future Planning and Advocacy.* Chicago: Rehabilitation Research and Training Center on Aging with Developmental Disabilities, Department of Disability and Human Development, University of Illinois at Chicago.

Heller, T., M. Janicki, J. Hammel, and A. Factor. 2002. *Promoting Healthy Aging, Family Support, and Age-Friendly Communities for Persons Aging with Developmental Disabilities: Report of the 2001 Invitational Research Symposium on Aging and Developmental Disabilities.* Chicago: Rehabilitation Research and Training Center on Aging with Developmental Disabilities, Department of Disability and Human Development, University of Illinois at Chicago.

Herr S., L. Gostin, and H. Koh, eds. 2003. *The Human Rights of Persons with Intellectual Disabilities.* New York and Oxford: Oxford University Press.

Holburn S., and P. Vietze. 2002. *Person-Centered Planning.* Baltimore: Paul H. Brookes Publishing.

Prasher V., and M. Janicki. 2002. *Physical Health of Adults with Intellectual Disabilities.* Oxford: Blackwell Publishing.

Schulzinger, R. 2003. *Family Resource Guide.* Silver Springs, MD: The Arc of the United States.

Stone, J. 1995. *Community Living Options: Family Funded, Individually Owned, or Shared.* Monograph No. 2, Rehabilitation Research and Training Center. Lexington, KY: Consortium on Aging with Mental Retardation, Interdisciplinary Human Development Institute, University of Kentucky.

References

Bouras N., and G. Holt. 2003. Community mental health support services. In *Mental Health, Intellectual Disabilities and the Aging Process*, eds. P. Davidson, V. Prasher, and M. Janicki, 199-209. Oxford: Blackwell Publishing.

Chen, S. C., S. Ryan-Henry, T. Heller, and E. Chen. 2001. Health status of mothers of adults with intellectual disability. *Journal of Intellectual Disability Research* 45(5):439-449.

Condon, C., L. Enein-Donovan, M. Gilmore, and M. Jordan. 2004. *When Existing Jobs Don't Fit: A Guide to Job Creation*. ICI Professional Development Series, Institute Brief 17. Available at www.communityinclusion.org/article.php?article_id=126.

Cooper, E., and A. O'Hara. 2003. *Regional Housing Forum: A Technical Assistance Guide for Housing Resources and Strategies*. Boston: Technical Assistance Collaborative. Available at www.shang.org/Resources/guide.htm.

Davis, S., ed. 2003. *A Family Handbook on Future Planning*. Chicago: The Arc of the United States and Rehabilitation Research and Training Center on Aging with Developmental Disabilities, Department of Disability and Human Development, College of Applied Health Sciences, University of Illinois at Chicago.

DeBrine, E., J. Caldwell, A. Factor, and T. Heller. 2003. *The Future Is Now: A Future Planning Training Curriculum for Families and Their Adult Relatives with Developmental Disabilities*. Chicago: Rehabilitation Research and Training Center on Aging with Developmental Disabilities, University of Illinois at Chicago.

Deshler, D., E. Ellis, and B. K. Lenz. 1996. *Teaching Adolescents with Learning Disabilities: Strategies and Methods*. Denver: Love Publishing Company.

Dowling, S., and S. Hollins. 2003. Coping with bereavement: The dynamics of intervention. In *Mental Health, Intellectual Disabilities and the Aging Process*, eds. P. Davidson, V. Prasher, and M. Janicki, 166-178. Oxford: Blackwell Publishing.

Dykens, E. 2005. Happiness, well-being, and character strengths: Outcomes for families and siblings of persons with mental retardation. *Mental Retardation* 43(5):360-363.

Fellman, W. 2000. *Finding a Career That Works For You.* Plantation, FL: Specialty Press.

Fujiura, G., and H. Park. 2003. *Demography of Aging Caretakers: Implications of the Greying of Family Households.* Chicago: Department of Disability and Human Development, University of Illinois at Chicago.

Greenbaum J. 1987. *Good Minds at Work: A Resource Manual for the "Science Abled" Video Program.* Ann Arbor, MI: The University of Michigan School of Dentistry.

Hartley, S. L., and W. E. MacLean. 2005. Perceptions of stress and coping strategies among adults with mild mental retardation: Insight into psychological distress. *American Journal of Mental Retardation* 110(4):285-297.

Hayden, M. F., and T. Heller. 1997. Support, problem solving/coping ability, and personal burden of younger and older caregivers of adults with mental retardation. *Mental Retardation* 35(5):364-372.

Heller, T., K. Hsieh, and L. Rowitz. 1997. Maternal and paternal caregiving of persons with mental retardation across the lifespan. *Family Relations* 46(4):407-415.

Markell, M. 2004. *Helping People with Developmental Disabilities Mourn: Practical Rituals for Caregivers.* Fort Collins, CO: Companion Press.

Markel, G., and J. Greenbaum. 1979. *Parents Are to Be Seen and Heard: Assertiveness in Education Planning for Handicapped Children.* San Luis Obispo, CA: Impact Press.

McCallion, P., and S. Kolomer. 2003. Psychosocial concerns among aging family carers. In *Mental Health, Intellectual Disabilities and the Aging Process*, eds. P. Davidson, V. Prasher, and M. Janicki, 179-195. Oxford: Blackwell Publishing.

National Organization on Disabilities/Harris Survey. 2000. *Executive Summary: 2000 NOD/Harris Survey of Americans with Disabilities.* Washington, DC: National Organization on Disabilities.

National Organization on Disabilities/Harris Survey. 2004. *NOD/Harris Survey of Americans with Disabilities.* Washington, DC: National Organization on Disabilities.

Nichols, P. 1996. *Clear Thinking: Clearing Dark Thoughts with New Words and Images.* Iowa City, IA: River Lights Publishers.

Powell, T., and P. Ogle. 1985. *Brothers and Sisters: A Special Part of Exceptional Families.* Baltimore: Paul H. Brooks Publishing.

President's Committee for People with Intellectual Disabilities. 2004. *A Charge We Have to Keep: A Road Map to Personal and Economic Freedom for Persons with Intellectual Disabilities in the 21st Century.* Available at www.acf.hhs.gov/programs/pcpid/2004_rpt_pres/2004_PCPID_Report.pdf.

Rizzolo, M. C., R. Hemp, D. Braddock, and A. Pomeranz-Essley. 2004. *The State of the States in Developmental Disabilities.* Boulder: University of Colorado, Coleman Institute for Cognitive Disabilities and Department of Psychiatry.

Seltzer, M., J. Greenberg, G. Orsmond, and J. Lounds. 2005. Life course studies of siblings of individuals with developmental disabilities. *Mental Retardation* 43(5):354-359.

Seltzer, M., and M. Krauss. 2002. *Aging with Autism and Mental Retardation: Challenges and Rewards of Caregiving by Older Parents and Adult Siblings.* Chicago: Rehabilitation Research and Training Center on Aging with Developmental Disabilities, Department of Disability and Human Development, University of Illinois at Chicago.

Seltzer M., M. Krauss, and S. Magana. 1998. *Family Involvement by Aging Parents and Adult Siblings with Individuals with Intellectual Disabilities Living in Residential Settings.* Chicago: Rehabilitation Research and Training Center on Aging with Developmental Disabilities, Department of Disability and Human Development, University of Illinois at Chicago.

Wehman, P. 2006. *Life Beyond the Classroom: Transition Strategies for Young People with Disabilities*, Fourth edition. Baltimore: Paul H. Brooks Publishing.

Judith Greenbaum, Ph.D., is the mother of an adult daughter with moderate to severe mental retardation. She currently consults with school districts and families on the development of appropriate educational environments for children with disabilities. She has worked with children and adults with disabilities for 35 years, and has spent much of her educational and professional career as an advocate for people with disabilities and their families. She has written numerous articles and presented many workshops and seminars for families, educators, social service workers, and mental health professionals on how to access community services, develop effective programs, and work with other educational and social services professionals to best care for and support developmentally disabled people. She earned her Ph.D. in Special Education at the University of Michigan.

more titles for children & adults with special needs from new**harbinger**publications

The Gift of ADHD

$14.95 • Item Code: 3899

Helping Your Child Overcome an Eating Disorder

$16.95 • Item Code: 3104

Helping Your Depressed Child

$15.95 • Item Code: 3228

Helping Your Child with Selective Mutism

$14.95 • Item Code: 416X

Helping a Child with Nonverbal Learning Disorder or Asperger's Syndrome

$14.95 • Item Code: 2779

Helping Your Child Overcome Separation Anxiety or School Refusal

$14.95 • Item Code: 4313

Helping Your Anxious Child

$14.95 • Item Code: 1918

Getting Help

$21.95 • Item Code: 4757

Helping Your Child with Autism Spectrum Disorder

$17.95 • Item Code: 3848

Helping Your Child with OCD

$19.95 • Item Code: 3325

available from new**harbinger**publications
and fine booksellers everywhere

To order, call toll free **1-800-748-6273** or visit our online bookstore at **www.newharbinger.com**
(V, MC, AMEX • prices subject to change without notice)